Building Modern Business Applications

Reactive Cloud Architecture for Java, Spring, and PostgreSQL

Peter Royal

Apress®

Building Modern Business Applications: Reactive Cloud Architecture for Java, Spring, and PostgreSQL

Peter Royal
Sherman Oaks, CA, USA

ISBN-13 (pbk): 978-1-4842-8991-4   ISBN-13 (electronic): 978-1-4842-8992-1
https://doi.org/10.1007/978-1-4842-8992-1

Managing Director, Apress Media LLC: Welmoed Spahr
Acquisitions Editor: Jonathan Gennick
Development Editor: Laura Berendson
Coordinating Editor: Jill Balzano

Cover Photo by Jorge Salvador on Unsplash

Distributed to the book trade worldwide by Springer Science+Business Media LLC, 1 New York Plaza, Suite 4600, New York, NY 10004. Phone 1-800-SPRINGER, fax (201) 348-4505, e-mail orders-ny@springer-sbm. com, or visit www.springeronline.com. Apress Media, LLC is a California LLC and the sole member (owner) is Springer Science + Business Media Finance Inc (SSBM Finance Inc). SSBM Finance Inc is a **Delaware** corporation.

For information on translations, please e-mail booktranslations@springernature.com; for reprint, paperback, or audio rights, please e-mail bookpermissions@springernature.com.

Apress titles may be purchased in bulk for academic, corporate, or promotional use. eBook versions and licenses are also available for most titles. For more information, reference our Print and eBook Bulk Sales web page at http://www.apress.com/bulk-sales.

Any source code or other supplementary material referenced by the author in this book is available to readers on GitHub (https://github.com/Apress). For more detailed information, please visit http://www. apress.com/source-code.

Printed on acid-free paper

To Tricia, without whose support over the years I wouldn't have arrived at a place where this book could happen.

Table of Contents

About the Author

Peter Royal is a practicing software developer with over 20 years of experience. A common thread has been working on business applications, whether they are tracking legal casework, domain-specific ERP suites, or financial trading and risk management. He enjoys building tools for his colleagues, working with them to meet their needs, and providing solutions that bring joy rather than frustration. He has come to appreciate pragmatic architectures and development practices that enable systems to thrive for the long term. He currently resides in Los Angeles, CA, with his wife, daughter, and cat.

About the Technical Reviewer

Alexandru Jecan is a software engineer and author. He is working at Deutsche Bank as Assistant Vice President in the area of investment banking. Alexandru also speaks at programming conferences across Europe and the United States.

Alexandru is the author of the book *Java 9 Modularity Revealed* (Apress) and the technical reviewer of the books *Java Program Design* (Apress) and *Jakarta EE Recipes* (Apress).

His book *Java 9 Modularity Revealed* was featured during the keynote speech by Mark Reinhold at the JavaOne Conference 2018 in San Francisco.

Alexandru lives with his wife Diana and his daughters Melissa and Mia in Berlin and is currently studying for the Project Management Certification.

You can reach Alexandru at `alexandrujecan@gmail.com`.

Acknowledgments

The ideas in this book are an amalgamation of concepts I have encountered over my career, many of whose attribution is lost to time. I value everyone that takes the time to write and share knowledge with others, knowing that they will never fully understand the reach that they have.

To John Caruso and Gary Foster, for without your support and trust early on in my career trajectory I would not have been here. To Paul Hammant, for being a source of ideas, inspiration, and encouragement. To all my friends from the Apache Software Foundation, especially the early Avalon and Cocoon communities, for being unknowing mentors and shaping how to think about problems. To Snehal Chenneru and Michael Li, for without your help and support we never would have built the system this book is about.

Practicing the art of Brazilian jiu-jitsu has shaped my perspectives on continuous learning, humility, and problem solving. To my teachers, Andre, Sandro, and Chris, your methods for sharing knowledge have shaped mine.

This book would not exist if it were not for Jonathan Gennick reaching out to me and asking me if I had ever thought about writing a book. You had the vision that there was something worth sharing in a more durable form than a conference talk. You and your team at Apress helped bring this book to fruition.

Trish, Poppy, and Pickles, thank you for your support while I spent nights and weekends writing. You are the best.

Introduction

One of the first jobs I had was at a consulting firm where we were assisting a client in how to modernize their software. The client had a successful business selling and supporting a domain-specific ERP (Enterprise Resource Planning) system. It dated back to the 1970s with code written in BASIC-2C targeting the Wang minicomputer. When I entered the picture in the late 1990s the software was running on Windows via an emulator, its text-based interface trapped in a window. The owner of the firm did not want to get locked into a proprietary platform again. In a very forward-thinking move, we were explicitly asked to create a web-based user interface and a Java-based backend.

As we incrementally migrated modules from the old system to the new one, we received user feedback around the usability of the new interface. The text-based interface of the old system allowed power users to quickly navigate around. The new graphical interface did not initially have the same capabilities. We added extensive keyboard shortcuts to make navigation easier, but the nature of the interface prevented us from matching the experience of the old system. Existing users valued the system as it was, while new customers were enticed by the new web-based interface.

This was an enlightening experience for me, how deeply the nature of my work affected the work of others, and how attached people can be to the familiar. I was attached to the familiar. While the new system we created used technologies and techniques that were more modern than what the old system used, the paradigms were fundamentally the same. In the two decades since I worked on that system, again the technologies and techniques have changed, but the same paradigms live on. As I made this observation and introspected the work I had done, I came to realize that there are other ways to build systems. That's what this book is about.

I start this book by defining and scoping business applications, and then my perspectives on the status quo. The next part discusses architectural precepts that I believe are appropriate for forward-looking systems and why business applications should be built with them in mind. Business applications encode business rules, and business rules can change over time. Understanding each of these is important, and I dedicate a chapter to each. The third part of this book is my proposal for a modern business application architecture. I describe my self-imposed constraints and the principles that the architecture aims to uphold. The architecture is described in detail, but from a conceptual and data flow perspective. The architecture may be implemented in your desired language. It has technological requirements, but you can choose implementations you are the most comfortable working with. There are production systems using this architecture, and the final part is about the implementation choices I made. The final chapter is about additions that can be made to the architecture as well as alternate means of implementation. My goal is to show that the architecture is really a starting point for systems, not the end state. Your systems will have their own lives and need to grow in ways that are unique to their environments.

You don't need to know any specific computer languages to understand this book. A familiarity with building systems is valuable, but also not required. I describe the *what*, not the *how*, as I believe the former will be more durable over time. As I learned early in my career, implementation decisions change, but paradigms endure.

Thank you for taking the time to read this book. I hope that my reasoning resonates with you. I would love to hear your stories of how you have taken the ideas from this book and applied them to your work.

—Pete

PART I

Business Applications

CHAPTER 1

What Is a Business Application?

"Modern Business Application" is a vague and imprecise term, conjuring up differing mental images for each individual. Before we embark upon our journey of building one, I need to ensure that you have an understanding of what I mean.

In this chapter I will introduce what a "Modern Business Application" is, for the purposes of this book. The progression of the book follows with the desired properties for business applications, how those properties can be manifested into the design of a system, and finishing with a discussion on implementation.

I feel a critical aspect in developing successful business software is understanding the business. The corollary for this book is understanding what a business application is, in order to understand what we will be building.

Business Software

In 2001, Watts S. Humphrey started off his book entitled *Winning with Software: An Executive Strategy*[1] with a chapter on "Why Every Business Is a Software Business." Ten years later, in 2011, Marc Andreessen wrote a piece[2] for *The Wall Street Journal* entitled "Why Software Is Eating the World." Fast-forward to 2019, and Microsoft's CEO Satya Nadella reaffirmed[3] Watts' declaration with "Every Company Is Now a Software Company" during a discussion at the Mobile World Congress.

---

[1] https://www.informit.com/store/winning-with-software-an-executive-strategy-9780201776393

[2] https://a16z.com/2011/08/20/why-software-is-eating-the-world/

[3] https://www.satellitetoday.com/innovation/2019/02/26/microsoft-ceo-every-company-is-now-a-software-company/

© Peter Royal 2023
P. Royal, *Building Modern Business Applications*, https://doi.org/10.1007/978-1-4842-8992-1_1

The increasing reliance that businesses place on software had been anticipated and has come to pass. Nearly all businesses rely on some form of "Commercial Off The Shelf" (COTS) software, even as the "shelf" is now commonly an "… as a service" offering.

Each business is unique, and their software needs reflect that. However, "software" is a broad term. This book is about a specific type of software, "applications." An "application" (or "app") is software for end users, whether they are a business's employees or customers. While all businesses benefit from software that is customized for how they operate, the incremental value to the business relative to what's available as COTS generally results in developers such as you and I working for larger organizations.

Let's break down the attributes that will comprise our definition of "Business Application."

Domain Specific

A business can be said to operate within a given industry. Industries are very broad domains, such as finance, manufacturing, entertainment, etc. At a certain size, they generally partition themselves into internal functional areas, or departments, such as sales, marketing, accounting, etc. While there are commonalities in a given department across all industries, the combination of industry and department yields many unique values, as no two businesses conduct themselves in an identical fashion. In fact, the way a business internally organizes itself can be an important differentiator. Having an internal organization that's different from its peers can be a competitive advantage.

This is our area of focus, applications that are tailored toward specific departments. Some departments, such as accounting, have enough similarity across domains to support third-party vendors. Often, such software will have the ability to be customized to adapt it to the unique specifics of a business. However, this comes with risks, as a critical component of a department's operation is now in the hands of a third party. This relationship has been recognized by financiers, some of whom acquire these vendors and slow improvements in the software in order to collect lucrative support fees, as without the software the business would falter.

A mitigation to that risk is for a business to hire or contract software developers such as yourself to create these applications. Having full control of the application allows the business to control its future. This is the basis for "every company being a software company." What once may have been a competitive advantage has now morphed into table stakes.

How It Is Used

Within this departmental domain, our business applications are ones that act as a source of truth for the department. The application is both the "system of record," in addition to the "system of engagement." It is the system that users interact with for data entry, as well as being the authoritative store for that data. In very large corporations, there may be a single corporate-wide system (an Enterprise Resource Planning system,[4] or ERP) that is the system of record, delegating the system of engagement to other systems. Those systems are far larger than the ones we are focusing on.

The most straightforward way to capture data into a system of record is to make it a job requirement for employees to use the system. Or, in the case of a customer-facing system, being the only way to interact with the business. It is important to have empathy for the users of these systems. As software developers, if there are annoyances with the tools we use daily, in many cases we can modify our tools to remove what's frustrating. For users of business applications where usage of it is a condition of performing their job, they do not have that luxury. The responsibility to ensure that using an application is, as a minimum, pleasant, falls to us. With information captured into an application, the business is then able to use the data in pursuit of its goals.

Data is not captured in a vacuum. Without structure, data can be worse than meaningless, creating additional confusion. Based on the business's current objectives, a structure for data can be devised, a model. The rigidity of this model can have a direct impact on the business's ability to adapt to changes in the future. If a change in the business requires a change in this model, the application that houses this model must then be updated for the business itself to change. Writing software in a manner that is amenable to change is valuable and can be under-appreciated. There is a balancing act between doing exactly what is required vs. generalizing based on what could change in the future. However, there are techniques that, to a degree, can side-step this balancing act by taking a different path entirely. We will discuss this more in Chapter 4.

---

[4] An ERP is a system that facilitates organizational-wide management of processes and data. They are frequently composed of modules that relate to facets of the business such as inventory management, purchase orders, and accounting. They are highly customizable to the needs of the business.

Business applications enforce processes and workflows. These workflows describe the activities that must be taken based on data in the system, without prescribing who performs them. By formalizing them into an application, adherence to them is increased or guaranteed. We are focusing on applications that allow users to collaborate on workflows. Our business applications are multiuser systems.

Collectively, requirements on the structure of data and the processes by which the data is modified are known as business rules. We will explore business rules in depth in Chapter 5.

Measuring Importance

As engineers, our view of an application's importance is often based on how it is used. An application that is frequently used and/or manages large amounts of data is important. These two dimensions are conflated when referring to the "scale" of an application. The larger the scale, the larger the importance. That may not be the business's perspective, however. Instead, it is the criticality of the application to the continued operation and success of the business's operations.

For purposes of this book, our data volume sweet spot is what I like to refer to as "medium-sized data" (as a play on the "big data" nomenclature that swept over tech in the early part of this century). Medium-sized data fits in the storage capacity of a single server, although multiple servers may be used for resiliency. The data may also fit entirely in memory, something that is increasingly true as system capacities increase, and the changing nature of storage systems. Think gigabytes, not terabytes.

As our business applications are targeted at end users, its access frequency will be at human-scale speeds. The number of users will be the driving factor in the overall number of requests, which will likely be measured in requests per minute rather than second. This has implications on how we observe the behavior of our systems; the sparser the requests, the trickier it becomes to use metrics to monitor its behavior. Is the system unavailable, or is it a quiet period for users? This is explored in Chapter 12.

An application that is important to the business must be available for use when the business requires it. There will likely be periods of time for the business in which the unavailability of the application would be disastrous. An application's sole purpose could be to assist users during these critical periods, as the formalization of the business processes performed with the application helps ensure they are performed as intended.

"Modern"

Modern is an adjective that will ultimately date whatever uses it. In using this label, we are certainly declaring that our techniques are more up to date than others. Computing capabilities have grown by leaps and bounds in the past two decades. It isn't that older techniques become invalid. Rather, increased compute and storage capacity have made new techniques viable. Techniques that may have only lived on a whiteboard are now able to be put into production use.

This is our modern, more akin to modern tools than modern art. In time, with your help, they will become the new status quo. There will certainly be techniques in the future that beget reuse of the modern label again, but such is the cycle of progress.

The techniques I describe and advocate for in this book are not novel. I am making the case that not only is it entirely feasible to use them but doing will lead to software applications that are better suited for the current moment and into the future.

"Cloud Computing" is an intriguing trend that both abstracts developers from the physical machine and can demand increased mechanical sympathy with the machine as a mechanism for controlling costs. It is easier than ever to provision compute resources, and inattention to the resources in use can invert the value proposition for a business.

I discuss this in concrete terms in Chapter 4. The techniques I will describe open up the possibility of managing consumed resources in closer concert with what is required at the time, even if it isn't acted upon. Similar to how I explain how to make an application's logic amenable to change, the same principle is extended to the resources required for operation.

Summary

The business applications this book referred to can be described thusly:

- Tailored to a specific domain

- Bespoke work, either performed by employee-developers or consultants

- Usage by employees is mandatory

- Multiuser

- Data entry and decision support are core functions

- A source of truth for the business

- Value is derived from workflow and decision analysis automation

- Medium-sized data

- Criticality is due to importance to the business

Modern is in relation to current development practices, which I discuss in the next chapter.

CHAPTER 2

The Status Quo (and How It Came to Be)

Now that we have established a definition of a business application, I'm going to discuss my perspective on the status quo and how it has come to be. It is based off of my observations of the industry over the past two decades, from the mid-1990s to the present day in 2021.

In this chapter I will describe the practices that I've observed in my career, and how I feel they may be improved. This will be a Java Virtual Machine (JVM) centric view, as that's where I've spent the majority of my career. That may be true for you, or could be, depending on where you are in your career arc. Let's dive in!

Business Application Architectures

While business application architectures have changed in the past 20 years, they have also largely remained the same. As developers, our systems repeat the same fundamental interaction patterns, albeit implemented with the technologies of the day. It is important to understand the past in order to understand the opportunities ahead.

The Status Quo

A "modern" business application likely presents itself as a web-based user interface. If it is recent enough it may be a single-page application, one where data is loaded in the background, and the page itself is dynamically rewritten. This is usually only window dressing. If you look closer, the page is probably firing off HTTP requests to a backend, passing JSON payloads back and forth. HTTP verbs will be used to coarsely describe the intended action, GET for retrieval, DELETE for removal, PUT to create, and POST to

9

update. Perhaps there is some thought to the URL schema, such as a version number, but probably not. It'll be a flat namespace of endpoints, like a bunch of functions in an unorganized namespace.

If you ask the developers what type of API they've created, they'll call it a "REST API," even though it's far from it. Slinging underspecified JSON back and forth with HTTP verbs isn't exactly what Roy Fielding described when he coined the term. I like to describe these APIs as "colloquial REST."

There are many frameworks, such as Rails, Django, and Spring, that assist with the mechanics of exposing the HTTP request to developers, such that a developer only needs to specify the URL, HTTP method, and the shape of the payload.

Once received, the request will undergo the appropriate validations and then an object-relational mapping (ORM) framework will be used to ultimately store or retrieve data from a relational database. The ORM framework is probably Hibernate, as it has garnered the lion's share of attention since its debut in 2001.

Relational databases are the workhorses of business applications, and for good reasons. The quality of software layers that exist between the database and the user means nothing if the database isn't capable of reliably storing and retrieving data. Relational databases have a well-specified and standardized mechanism for interacting with them, the Structured Query Language, SQL. As difficult as it may be to introduce any new technology into a business, it is even more difficult to introduce a new primary data storage system. As our business applications are important to the business, this leads to risk aversion around the choice of data store. This is why the choice of data store is *not* something I'm proposing innovating upon. I've been using PostgreSQL for a large part of my career, and it has always worked, and continues to be improved. It is why I'm advocating for using PostgreSQL as part of this book. If you have a different preferred database, continue to use that. You have hard-won operational knowledge that is worth retaining.

The schema used in the database is probably mostly reasonable, depending on the nature of the changes the business has asked upon the software over its lifetime, as well as the number of developers that have worked on it. One thing that is very likely to be true is that the application mutates data in place. As data changes, what it used to be is gone. Sometimes, there's an explicit business requirement for an "undelete" operation or tracking changes to specific fields. As this requires extra development work, it is usually omitted unless explicitly called out.

As a pithy summary, a "modern" business backend in Java is underspecified JSON exchanged via a colloquial REST API that mutates data in place in a relational database via Hibernate.

Green Screen

The first business applications I was exposed to were "green screen" applications. The term was a throwback to terminals that were connected to a central computer with multiple displays and keyboards (terminals), rather than networking computers. The terminals were often green CRT screens (thus the name) and had limited functionality. They could display text from the central computer, relay input back, and perhaps printing functionality. If you've configured a terminal in Linux, you may have seen references to these devices in potential values for the TERM environment variable such as vt100.

As personal computers became common, hardware terminal emulators were replaced by software terminal emulators running under Windows, the common desktop operating system at the time. This is where I was exposed to them, applications that the business depended upon that were more important than the lifecycle of the hardware that they were originally developed for. Hardware terminals had been replaced with desktop software, and central computers with a local area network.

Some of these systems are still in active use. They are written in languages that are now considered legacy, such as COBOL or RPG. Rewriting these systems in another language is a large effort and introduces risk to the business. Being an economic decision, the business risk due to errors in a migrated system is mitigated by continuing to use the old system and managing the risk of staffing the teams that maintain them. If you squint your eyes hard enough, you can view the manner in which these systems render output in a terminal as a baroque text-based protocol. There are products that take this approach and allow the creation of web-based user interfaces for them.

I am mentioning these applications as they are true "thin client" architectures. The client devices, terminals, could do little more than input and output. There were no facilities to run logic "client side" on terminals.

Rich Client

Popularized by Microsoft Access and Visual Basic (VB), a Rich Client is an application that is installed on a user's machine and connects to a central application over a local area network. In many situations, the central application was a relational database. Local area networks hadn't yet standardized on TCP/IP, and creating custom protocols wasn't a straightforward task. A sufficiently complex system may have used CORBA, a technology for performing method calls across languages and machines. The simplest way to create a multiuser application was to rely on a database server's wire protocol and use it as the server portion of an application.

Access and VB provided a visual experience for building user interfaces. This allowed those with little traditional programming experience to build simple applications to store and retrieve data. Microsoft provided a robust set of built-in UI widgets along with third-party vendors that sold widgets with additional functionality. Building multiuser business applications was straightforward, and the results behaved similarly to other desktop software. Being a discrete application on a user's machine also meant being able to directly interact with other tools, such as Excel or Word.

However, there was a big catch for developers, distributing their software. Applications weren't a single file to install. Shared libraries needed to be copied to particular locations on machines. If there were conflicts, the results could be extremely difficult to debug. The term "DLL hell" was coined to refer to this pain.

Rich clients offered users an excellent experience. This came at the cost of operational difficulties. The best user experience is worth nothing if the software won't run on your machine.

The Model-View-Controller (MVC) architectural pattern was an insight on how to segregate responsibilities in graphical user interfaces. Access and VB didn't offer strict adherence to this pattern. The relational database could be considered the model, and each display window (a form in their parlance) was similar to a combined view and controller.

Web Applications

Concurrent with rich clients, the web was invented. As the 1990s came to a close, TCP/IP became the de-facto protocol for local area networks, as it solved LAN communication in addition to internet access. This opened the possibility of running a web server on the LAN with users accessing an "intranet."

While the initial user experience was poor in comparison to rich clients, it simplified the lives of developers as there was no software to install on users' machines. Solving the operational pains of DLL hell was of value to IT departments.

The first web applications were page-based, harkening back to the document-centric view that the web started with. There were two developments that I feel led to the floodgates of web applications.

The first was a pause in revisions of the HTML specification. Through the 1990s the W3C released HTML 2, 3, and eventually 4. HTML 4 was initially released in last 1997, with a final revision as 4.01 in late 1999. It was almost nine years until the process for HTML 5 began.

While this was a stagnation in the specification, it was also a period of stability. I believe this stability provided a stable foundation to build applications upon.

The second important development was what is now known as XMLHTTPRequest, or XHR. This was a technique for communicating with the web server without a full page reload, allowing web applications to have interaction paradigms that began to mimic rich clients. A proprietary feature of Microsoft's Internet Explorer browser allowed JavaScript running in the browser to access components installed on the system through a technology known as ActiveX. This was a descendant of the same technology, COM, that Visual Basic used for its interface building. It was through this path that a component Microsoft had developed as part of their Outlook Web Access (allowing web-based access to a corporate email server) could be used on any page. Once this technique was discovered, it became a de-facto standard and was implemented in other browser engines.

With a stable specification and the ability to communicate with a server in the background, it was possible to build business applications that were "good enough" for daily use. Some business applications would continue to demand rich clients, as their requirements could not be met by a web-based application. However, if a web browser's capabilities were sufficient for an application, the operational ease of a web application made it the simpler long-term choice.

Frameworks that assisted developers in writing the application servers that backed these web-based applications converged upon the MVC pattern for structuring themselves. The model is no longer the database itself; it is an object model in the application server that's mapped to the database with an ORM. Code is organized into classes named controllers, with their response payloads being views. This was the genesis of the status quo that remains.

It is here that I believe web-based business applications have stagnated. While there have been continuing developments in the web that I discuss in the next section, by and large, the requirements of many business applications have been satisfied. The way in which the browser-side portion of an application is developed has changed, but the underlying browser primitives they use have not.

The Rise of Consumer Applications

Through the 2000s, if you wanted to use a website, you had to use a web browser on a desktop (or laptop) computer. This was the decade where broadband Internet access at home increased rapidly. Along with it was the "Web 2.0" movement that ushered in increased interactivity on websites, something that was made possible by the availability of XHR in browsers. Websites aimed at users flourished, and their activities online expanded beyond the transactional interactions that were similar to business applications.

In 2007, a shockwave rippled through the technology industry when Apple released the first iPhone. It allowed one to browse the web on a handheld device with pages rendering the same as they would on a desktop. Apple's initial plans were to have all user-installable applications be websites, but they backed away from that and allowed developers to write native applications delivered via the App Store. A new name for applications arrived, "apps." Google's Android mobile operating system quickly matched what Apple had done with an app store of their own.

This complicated the lives of UI developers targeting consumers. Previously, they had to deliver a website that was functional on the major desktop browser engines. Assumptions could be made around the available input devices (keyboard and mouse), approximate screen sizes, pixel density, and even the nature of their connection to the internet (stable latencies and packet loss, even though bandwidth varied due to broadband availability). With this mobile explosion, there were a myriad of screen sizes, the mouse replaced with touch interactions, a network with variable latency, and packet loss. There was, at least, a common browser engine, Apple's WebKit. One deliverable, a desktop website, had morphed into four: a desktop website, a mobile website, an iOS app, and an Android app. To help limit the number of targets, some native mobile applications embedded browser views to provide some of their functionality.

To allow mobile websites to have app-like capabilities, browser innovation began again with the addition of new features. Web workers allowed background execution, SSE for data pushed from the server, and WebSockets for a persistent bidirectional connection.

There was a Cambrian Explosion in the JavaScript ecosystem of frameworks making use of these new APIs, and overall streamlining of the development experience. A new pattern for delivering data emerged, GraphQL.

GraphQL provides a mechanism for an API caller to specify exactly what data they wish to have returned. This was a valuable feature when delivering data over a mobile network. It is a different paradigm from the MVC-style APIs that came before. To help bridge between older web APIs and the APIs desired by mobile clients, the Backend for the Frontend (BFF) pattern emerged. This is a service that acts as an adapter between existing APIs and the desired experience of the client.

Innovations in a user's experience (UX) also took place. Mobile device adoption accelerated after the iPhone and Android releases, and an app's ease-of-use became a valuable differentiator in the marketplace. New paradigms were invented in apps and percolated through the ecosystem (pull-to-refresh, not *needing* to refresh, notifications, infinite scrolling, and social collaboration, to name a few).

Previously, the difference between a business application delivered via the web and a consumer website was largely one of scale and audience. With the advent of mobile, consumer websites weren't mere websites, they also had to deliver an app experience. The set of skills needed to work on consumer experiences had expanded.

Thus, my assertion on the status quo. Prior to this mobile explosion, business applications and consumer websites could largely be built in a similar fashion. Why haven't business applications kept pace? I have some theories.

First, for new business applications, features that are common in apps are now taken for granted, and thus not explicitly called out by product managers when writing requirements, the same way that business-specific features are. The refresh/reload button is my favorite example here. Websites that automatically update their data have been possible since the invention of XHR. As a UX paradigm, it wasn't until the mobile explosion that it became common. If the refresh button were used, the browser may re-request assets that haven't changed in addition to the data that has. To streamline the experience, refresh moved into the app, and eventually disappeared. Instead, the content is kept up-to-date automatically. If a feature is invisible and omni-present, it becomes easier to miss when explicitly enumerating requirements.

Second, a lack of developer experience. As the set of skills needed to work on consumer experiences expanded, it creates a bifurcation in skillsets. One may have needed exposure to systems that utilized new browser capabilities to suggest their incorporation.

Finally, architectural impedance. It may not be straightforward to "bolt on" a change stream in order to have live updating pages or trigger notifications for a user. This gets to the heart of the remainder of this book. I'll be introducing a different way of building systems in the third part of this book that solves this impedance and will hopefully set a standard for the next phase of computing. The MVC pattern has served us well, but there is another step forward we can take. As we prepare to do so, there are other practices that are valuable to incorporate into our work.

Concurrent Practices

The practices involved in delivering software have also been evolving. A software architecture is more than how the pieces fit together, it's also how the pieces come together, how they are changed over time, how they are validated, and how their production performance is evaluated. In this section, I go over some practices that I believe are valuable for the long-term success of an application.

Agile

When the agile manifesto[1] was unveiled in 2001, it was a large shift in the way in which delivering software was thought about on a wide scale. I remember first reading it and it was as if a lightbulb had gone off in my head. It succinctly describes some of the pressures that software teams face and offers an extremely loose framework for thinking about them.

The act of constructing software isn't bound by the same physical constraints as constructing physical objects. I believe it is important to lean into that differentiation and use it to create better software. Software is, ultimately, an arrangement of bits. We have constructed fantastical systems to ease the process of arranging them just-so.

The point from the manifesto that stuck out to me the most was being amenable to change. To change software is to spend time doing so; there are no materials lost in the process. I have a strong belief that a key principle in building a system is that it needs to be amenable to change, and that will be reflected in what we build in the remainder of this book.

The manifesto also speaks to the processes around making changes. As mentioned in the first chapter, our business applications are a bespoke creation for the business. It is important for developers to view themselves as collaborators with the business, not contractors (even if the actual relationship is via a consultancy).

The *goal* of a business application is to help the business, and the agile manifesto describes how to approach those interactions.

---

[1] https://agilemanifesto.org/

Test-Driven Development

Test-driven development, or TDD, emerged from the agile practice of eXtreme Programming, or XP. Ken Beck "rediscovered[2]" the technique in the 1990s and wrote about it in his 1999 book *Extreme Programming Explained.*[3]

The crux of the idea is to write tests for functionality prior to implementing the functionality itself. At first, the test should run and fail, as the functionality hasn't been implemented. From then on, the goal is to make the test pass.

I've found this practice to be immensely valuable, as it puts me in the position of being a consumer of my code prior to writing it. The act of writing the test helps focus on what's important from an API perspective, and how the code should communicate with the rest of the codebase. I feel it helps create code that is easier to maintain as well. The act of writing a test before implementation somehow leads to a more thoughtful design. That design is more amenable to future change. I'm certain the fact that the code has tests helps maintainability, as changes can be made with confidence. However, I've found that there is a difference between code that had tests written prior to implementation and tests after. Empirically, I've seen it work and have become a believer in the practice. Tests need to be written regardless to validate that code works, so why not write them first?

Continuous Integration and Delivery

Continuous Integration and Continuous Delivery, CI/CD, are two more XP practices. They are distinct yet interrelated. When combined, they formalize the delivery pipeline for software. CI has become a standard practice. If your project utilizes a build server that compiles your project and runs tests after code pushes, you are practicing CI. To move into CD, the build server should also package the software up for deployment, perhaps even automating the deployment itself.

When practiced together, CI/CD allows you to push a change to your repository, and without any additional manual intervention have it running in your test environment. This can also be extended to promote builds into production automatically, although most business environments that I've worked in have preferred to have a human in the loop for that part, even if it is the simple act of clicking a button.

---

[2] https://www.quora.com/Why-does-Kent-Beck-refer-to-the-rediscovery-of-test-driven-development-Whats-the-history-of-test-driven-development-before-Kent-Becks-rediscovery

[3] ISBN13 978-0321278654

I find value in these practices as they complete the feedback loop. The test environment that exists on a build server is not the same as a deployed environment. This "pipeline" approach for delivering the software itself will be echoed in how we will be structuring the internals of our modern business application. There is also an element of a philosophical thought experiment here, akin to "If a tree falls in a forest and no one is around to hear it, does it make a sound?" – "If the software was changed but it was never deployed, was it ever really changed?". One refrain I will keep coming back to is that an application should be amenable to change. Easily getting those changes into the hands of users is crucial to this goal.

Observability

Observability is a trendy word. It comes from control theory, a measure of how well the internal states of a system can be inferred from its external outputs. In the late 2010s, it started to be applied to what could be generally coined the "monitoring" space.

As software developers, we've always been practicing this. We use the outputs of a system, such as log messages, to build an understanding of what is taking place inside. In the simplest sense, "practicing observability" means ensuring that your systems are emitting enough information that you can reconstruct what they are doing. This has always been a best practice, but I found implementations to be ad-hoc and on a case-by-case basis.

Formalizing this practice has increased in importance as our applications are increasingly not acting alone. They are a part of a larger ecosystem of applications that power a business. There is value in having applications emit these outputs in a common fashion, so problems can be debugged across applications.

The value I've found in this practice has been changing my mindset on how to approach debugging problems. Ideally, I do not want to have to use a debugger, nor add print statements to figure out the cause of a problem. I've tried to make it a goal to build systems such that they naturally emit enough information to mentally work through what the possible causes are, and then use a test to validate the hypothesis. It is another practice that will seep into how your software is structured, and how we will be structuring our modern business applications.

Summary

The manner in which business applications are architected hasn't substantially changed. The business and consumer applications were similar until the introduction of the iPhone, which begat many changes in consumer apps that haven't had wide adoption in business applications. Other development practices may have been incorporated into your workflow, as they are somewhat orthogonal to an application's architecture.

I feel there's an opportunity to fully incorporate technologies from consumer apps and practices from agile into a modern business application design.

In the next part of this book, I will further describe the desired properties and features of our design prior to the design itself in the third part.

PART II

Design Prerequisites

CHAPTER 3

What Is a Reactive System?

I've explained what a business application is and how they're currently built. In this chapter, I will investigate properties and features that are both essential and desired in their architecture. I start by defining what "reactive" is, followed by the idea of a reactive system, which is born from the properties laid out in the Reactive Manifesto.[1]

This chapter is about reactive systems in the large. The next chapter will investigate why build a business application as a reactive system.

What Is Reactive?

You have likely used a reactive system without realizing it: a spreadsheet. When you change the value in a cell in a spreadsheet, any formulas that reference that cell are automatically recomputed. And if those formula cells are then referenced, the process repeats. It is a straightforward and powerful idea.

To introduce a reactive system, we will first discuss reactive programming. After all, a system is the projection of programming concepts at a wider scale. There are two broad paradigms for programming, imperative and declarative.

Imperative is what you likely do on a day-to-day basis in a language such as Java. Each expression in the language is an instruction on what to do. When the program is being executed, it is following those instructions.

Declarative is the opposite. Rather than expressing what to do, the program is a specification of what we want to happen. If you have been introduced to functional programming concepts, you have been introduced to a form of declarative programming.

---

[1] www.reactivemanifesto.org/

© Peter Royal 2023
P. Royal, *Building Modern Business Applications*, https://doi.org/10.1007/978-1-4842-8992-1_3

The basis for reactive programming is thinking in data flows. The visual metaphor I use in my head is plumbing. Not necessarily what you'd find in the real world, but the game genre where you're presented with puzzles and the goal of matching specified faucets and drains.

That metaphor carries over to the expression of a program. The faucets, inputs, are the requests the program receives. The drains, outputs, are not only the responses to those requests, but also log statements, captured metrics, and even writing to a database.

Reactive programming is then the expression of a problem in that form. Inputs and outputs are connected, and the reactive runtime ensures that the "data is flowing" through our metaphorical pipes.

Of course, any real system isn't a direct connection of inputs to outputs. There will be splits, merges, and even feedback cycles in the flow. The key is that we are focused on the *what* rather than the *how*.

These are not new concepts. Dataflow programming was first conceived in the 1960s, and with the introduction of the VisiCalc spreadsheet program in 1979, a reactive environment was available on a PC.

Reactive programming is concerned with a single process. A reactive system is a composition of programs, composed in a reactive manner. A synchronous remote procedure call can be viewed as "imperative," whereas two programs communicating via a message bus can be viewed as "reactive." This is a very coarse generalization, but hopefully sufficient to illustrate the distinction.

In the next section, I'll discuss the Reactive Manifesto, a document that makes the case for reactive systems. As part of the discussion, I will further explain what makes up a reactive system.

Reactive Manifesto

In 2014, Jonas Bonér, Dave Farley, Roland Kuhn, and Martin Thompson unveiled the Reactive Manifesto. The underlying concepts had been percolating throughout the industry for a number of years. Similar to how the Agile Manifesto discussed in the prior chapter put a label on a collection of programming practices, the Reactive Manifesto is labeling architectural features of software systems.

I spoke to the rise of web applications in the prior chapter. For popular business and consumer services, those applications are operating at very large scales. Scale aside, the manner in which they were running also undertook a shift after the Amazon's Web

Services was introduced in 2006. The idea of a virtualized environment had been around for a number of years, VMWare had popularized it in the enterprise with its ESX product from the early 2000s. Amazon's product made virtual machines available to anyone and kicked off modern "cloud computing."

The manifesto was an aggregation of architectural practices that were common across systems in this new world. It is centered around four properties that I'll discuss in turn.

Responsive

The Oxford dictionary definition of responsive is "reacting quickly and positively." It is thus suiting that it is a property for reactive systems, given that the term itself is about reacting. The manifesto defines this property as *"[that] the system responds in a timely manner if at all possible."* This can be thought of as a reasonable maximum upper bound on how long to respond to a request or perform some action. A system that is responsive will prioritize consistent response times. In practice, this would mean something such as using internal timeouts, and responding with a timeout rather than appearing to hang.

Users *really* appreciate responsivity. Research on human and user interface response times has established that 250ms is a reasonable target. Google, Amazon, and Akamai have all done studies illustrating how users will abandon slow-loading websites. As we've established, usage of a business application isn't necessarily voluntary, but the overall point still stands. A slow application will lead to dissatisfied users.

The benefits aren't only to users, but to you, the operator of the system. The response time of a system can be incorporated into a Service Level Objective (SLO). A simple example is declaring that a percentage of all requests are replied to within a given timeframe. Enforcement of this can be done by a timeout in the system to respond with an error message if it would exceed the timeout. This can then be tied into an alert, giving feedback when the system may be under duress.

This can also establish a virtuous feedback loop. By being aware of the responsivity of the system, it can be tracked over time and improved. This can increase engagement and confidence in the system which is aligned with the business's goals of investing in the application.

Response times can also be a point of pride for developers. You can go to sleep at night knowing that your application isn't causing users to complain about waiting on the computer.

Resilient

Failures will happen. Being resilient is about remaining responsive when that occurs. You may have heard the idea of *"any sufficiently complex system is always in a state of partial failure."* Existing in that state and responding as if nothing is wrong is resiliency.

As a metaphor, think of bulkheads, especially on ships. A bulkhead helps partition the hull into multiple compartments, so should there be a breach of the hull, only that one compartment fills with water rather than the entire hull. Ideally, this will prevent, or at least slow, the sinking of the ship.

This same idea can be applied to software. Each logical component of your system should be able to experience failure without affecting other components. Another manifestation would be the ability to restart the database without needing to restart applications that connect to it. The failure, inability to connect to the database, is transient, and the applications that connect to it automatically recover.

This plays into responsiveness, as if a required dependency is experiencing failure, an error is propagated rather than hanging a request while waiting for recovery.

While some amount of resiliency can be "bolted on" to an existing application, I believe that to be truly resilient, it must be an intentional facet of the architecture.

Elastic

Elasticity. Like the word itself, it's applicability can be stretched in various dimensions. In the context of the manifesto, it is referring to the ability to remain responsive. The system has a level of self-awareness around target response times and is able to dynamically increase the resources it is using in order to maintain the target. Conversely, it is able to relinquish resources that are no longer necessary.

In the simple case, this is the automation of horizontal scaling. A more complex form could be the automation of data shards.

Out of all the properties, this is the most complex to utilize. It is entirely possible that you may never need to realize this property in your system. However, like resiliency, this must be an intentional facet of the architecture.

I think of this in two ways. The first is runtime elasticity, the ability to remain responsive as the workload of the system changes. The second is design elasticity, the ability to enable runtime elasticity as the system evolves.

To reuse the pipe metaphor, when thinking of how data (or requests for data) flow through your system, be cognizant of where a tee could be inserted to split or join the flow. Your system may never require the injection of the tees. Consideration of where they would go establishes logical boundaries in your design and provides a path toward runtime elasticity. Even though it may never be used, establishing those boundaries results in a design that is easier to communicate and reason about.

Message Driven

This is my favorite property, as well as the most important. Our metaphorical pipes don't contain a continuous stream. The stream is atomized into discrete messages.

Messages already exist in your system, that's how it receives its inputs. The Internet is a packet-switched network; packets are messages. Any higher-level abstraction is ultimately composed of messages.

Abstracting a sequence of messages into a continuous stream has its uses, such as the exchange of large files. I believe its valuable to defer this abstraction until it is really needed, which for our business applications, may never occur. Retaining control over the flow of discrete messages gives us units that can be explicitly managed.

Messages themselves aren't enough, it is the way they are exchanged, *asynchronously*. It is the combination of *asynchronous* **and** *message passing* that is key to this property.

Synchronous execution of code is an illusion on modern computers. We will eschew that fiction and embrace the reality that our code doesn't need to block and wait for a response, we gain control over how failures are managed. We can represent them as more messages.

In passing messages asynchronously, a boundary is introduced behind which implementation details can be abstracted.

Imagine sending an HTTP request to a server identified by a DNS name. When making the request, you don't know, or frankly care, where the receiving server is located. All that ultimately matters is the receipt of a response.

It is the same principle that is applied to the communication into and inside of our system. This is *location transparency*. A component is not concerned with where the recipients of its messages reside. They could be co-located in the same process, another process on the same machine, or somewhere else entirely. This allows for flexibility in the systems architecture. A component can move about without disrupting how callers interact with it.

If you have experience with the Spring Framework, or more broadly Dependency Injection, you have been introduced to this idea. Dependency injection is when a given component in a system doesn't have fixed references to other components that it collaborates with. Instead, other components that it requires, are injected by a control plane, or a framework such as Spring.

Dependency Injection is a specialization of a more general idea, inversion of control.[2] Rather than a component controlling its dependencies, it has relinquished that to the control plane. The goal is isolation of the component, and dependency injection is a means of achieving that.

Asynchronous message passing is also a form of control inversion. Rather than injecting classes or interfaces that are needed, communication channels, our pipes, are injected.

In using this mechanism to communicate between components, we are establishing bulkheads for resiliency. They are also points where a tee can be injected for elasticity. We are also creating points for observing the system. By observing the messages passed between components, we can gain an understanding of how the system is behaving.

If a component is receiving messages faster than it can process them, it can apply back-pressure. Back-pressure is a feedback mechanism where a message consumer can indicate to the producer that they are unable to accept additional message. This allows the producer to decide how to handle the situation, can be a signal for implementing elasticity, or shedding load in order to maintain resiliency.

Composing a Reactive System

A beauty I find in a reactive system is that it can be "turtles all the way down." In having a uniform method for components to communicate, via asynchronous message passing, this location transparency allows for the system to evolve without major changes. A component can start its life in-process with other components that it collaborates with. Over time, perhaps there's a need for that component to live on another machine. It's not a breaking change to its collaborators, as the means with which they communicate is the same. Nothing is free, perhaps there will be new latency concerns, or a new class of failures that need to be handled, but the basic principle stands.

---

[2] https://web.archive.org/web/20040202120126/
http:/www.betaversion.org/~stefano/linotype/news/38/

The metaphor of interlocking bricks such as the popular LEGO™ brand line has been long used for the composition of components in a modular software architecture. While I find value in this metaphor with its brick-centric view of how components can be easily "snapped together" to achieve a goal, the metaphor minimizes what has made LEGO™ bricks an enduring toy: the uniformity of how they connect.

To push this analogy further, during my formative years when I'd pass time building with my LEGO™ bricks, intermixed with our official parts were a handful of Tyco Super Blocks. Tyco's bricks were nominally compatible with LEGO™, but they didn't fit together the same as the genuine parts.

From a functionality standpoint of being a brick that supported my creation, they were functional. But, since they failed in the *interface uniformity*, they were often a weak point in a larger design.

This is the similarity with a reactive system. By having a uniform interface for communication between components, the resulting system is stronger, more resilient, by virtue of that decision.

Each interconnection between components in your system is an extension point where the data flow may be manipulated, whether it is to increase elasticity or provide additional resiliency. The extension point exists, even if goes unused. Since the extension point is due to the uniform interface, any cost associated with it has been amortized across the codebase. As it was not created solely for this location in the code, it approaches the ideal of a zero-cost feature.

Whether turtles or bricks, the uniformity is in how each component behaves when observed externally, following and guided by these properties of a reactive system.

Summary

These four properties define a reactive system. It is one that relies on asynchronous message passing for communication, which helps enable elasticity and resiliency, all in the service of remain responsive to its users. The act of passing messages is a form of a data flow, a long-standing technique in programming.

In the next chapter, we will discuss why design a business application as a reactive system.

CHAPTER 4

Why Build Business Applications As Reactive Systems?

We now have a shared understanding of what defines a business application, and what is a reactive system. In this chapter, we will explore the benefits of building business applications as reactive systems. As a part of defining a business application, we touched on a business's expectations from the application. I will start this chapter by expanding upon those expectations, as well as your expectations as a developer. I will then again go through the four properties of a reactive system, and explicitly relate them to business and developer expectations. After that, you will know the answer to the question posed in the title: Why build business applications as reactive systems?

Business Expectations

In the first chapter, as part of scoping our definition of a business application, I described how the application is used by the business as a key component. In thinking of what the business *expects* from the application, it is more than the mechanics as to how it is used.

In acting as a system of record for the business, there is an expectation that the application will be available when the business needs to store or retrieve data. If the business grows in a dimension such as the number of employees, or order volume, the application is expected to continue to meet its needs. If a business workflow needs to be adjusted, changing the application to enforce the change should not be a limiting factor.

© Peter Royal 2023
P. Royal, *Building Modern Business Applications*, https://doi.org/10.1007/978-1-4842-8992-1_4

I would broadly describe this as: the business expects the application to be available when required and is able to respond to changes in business needs in a timely fashion. I hope that this is somewhat self-evident, as it is the kernel of the relationship between any service provider and the party that subscribes to their services. It is a simple expectation. The complexity lies in making it happen.

Our business applications are written by developers like yourself, either as employees or consultants. The business's expectations for its applications are, transitively, expectations on how you build and make the application available to the business.

Developer Expectations

You are a user of your application as well! I think this is important to state explicitly. You likely aren't using the same interface as other users, but you are a user, nonetheless. Your primary interface is the application's source code. Secondarily, build and deployment pipelines, and tools used to monitor application health and behavioral observation.

You expect the code to be straightforward to work with. I use this term rather than easy, as there will be inherit complexity in your domain. Ideally, this is the sole source of complexity. Anything beyond that has been unnecessarily created and has the opportunity for minimization. That is one of the goals of this book, to provide a guide for building business applications that reduces unnecessary complexity. If the methods here seem complex, I postulate that is because they may be foreign.

In reducing complexity, that does not mean that the need for expertise is also reduced. When we build applications, we are in effect building machines. The methods in this book are a different, and I believe better, way of building those machines. I am imparting some of my experience to help your understanding in the journey of building your expertise.

The business's expectations for its applications are transitively applied to you, as you turn those expectations into reality. As a part of this, you will be operating within constraints. Ultimately, they can be broken down into two forms, time and money.

Time can be represented as money. There is a price that would allow anyone imposing a time constraint to allow more time, but that's generally the infeasible solution. For practical purposes, especially in our context, treating them as independent is simpler. Entertaining this line of thought is a topic unto itself, one that this book is not specifically about. I characterize it as a sort of systems thinking. If you have exposure to, or read further on the topic, you may see how our reactive systems are conceptually aligned.

The business is deriving economic value from the application. If the application is creating a deficit, costing more to operate than the value returned, the application's sustainability will be called into question. I find it important as developers to be cognizant of this situation. The relationships with coworkers required to build this understanding are also beneficial in understanding the business itself, which is useful domain knowledge when implementing business rules.

The monetary cost is often a direct calculation. There are hardware and software resources used for development and operation, plus salaries for the staff. While important, I believe operating costs are of lesser importance. They tend to move in a more predictable fashion relative to a planning horizon. Given a two, five, or even ten-year plan, there is sufficient hard data to make an informed prediction. Moore's Law and the general trend for computing costs have a dampening effect on the margin of error.

Time is key. This comes in two variations. Businesses will try and "buy time" by increasing staffing. The negative outcomes of this have been well captured by The Mythical Man-Month, and with Brooke's Law, *"Adding manpower to a late software project makes it later."* Embedded in this idea, that more individuals will allow a project to come to completion faster, is the notion that it is the ability to effectively change the software that is a limiting factor. If the business wants to change its operations, there is an opportunity cost if the software can't also change in a timely manner.

I've found that this idea, how *amenable to change* an application is, is directly related to a developer's interface to the application, it's source code. Expressed in the source is the *structure of the application*. If a system is not amenable to change, changes will take more time to perform. By being able to change faster, we are in effect, buying time. You may have been exposed to this idea before, under the guise of "good code" or "clean code." Those same sentiments still apply. In my experience, they often describe concepts abstractly, rather than providing specific guidance. That is wholly understandable, as they're guiding principles, rather than a specific architecture. In this book, I'm providing specifics for that architecture. A reactive system provides a holistic architecture, one that is composable, so what applies in the large applies in the small, and vice versa.

Property Alignment

Mirroring the prior chapter, I will go through each property in turn, relating how it is aligned with both the business and developer expectations of the system. I will refer to the two constraints mentioned under developer expectations, time and money, from the perspective of the business as well. While working within those constraints is an expectation of a developer, the management of time and money is of value to the business.

Responsive

If you've ever been on the phone with someone and they've had to apologize for their slow computers, you've been on the receiving end of the value of this. It's true, "time is money," and having users unnecessarily wait can be a drag. This can have a multiplicative effect. It isn't only the direct users of an application that may be hampered by slow response times, anyone that the users are helping is affected as well.

As developers, this is a tricky one to value. If asked directly as to how responsive a system should be, users will often give a vague answer that it should "be fast." It is often straightforward for users to identify what is unacceptable, but the inverse is highly subjective. Performance optimization work is notoriously open-ended, making it difficult to plan around.

My key takeaway on being responsive is in the establishment of an upper bound of acceptability. This removes the ambiguity of "is it slow, or is it stuck" when diagnosing failures. An upper bound on responsiveness also provides a starting point for discussing and planning for response time improvements.

An application's users appreciate responsive applications, and developers will find them easier to operate. This is the most user-visible property and executing it well can help establish a positive feedback cycle with the business where they build trust in the application and it's developers to provide the system to them in a timely manner.

Resilient

Failures will happen, planned or unplanned. If you don't plan to handle failure gracefully, it won't be. Gracefully handling failure reduces the operational toil on the system. By minimizing the impact of a failure, the recovery time can be decreased, restoring service quickly and safely. The business expects the application to be there when it needs it, and resiliency is the means to make that happen. In the user's eyes, is system being "up," being available.

In a broader view, being resilient is about handling *unexpected system states*. If a component fails, it is unexpected, otherwise the failure would have been handled.

There is also an expected system state that developers put the system in that may result in the system being unavailable, **deployments**.

A deployment can be seen as a transition between two states, the state in which the system is running the old and new code. The frequency of this depends on how often deployments occur. If you are practicing continuous delivery, this could occur, well, continuously. There is another dimension to a deployment depending on how it occurs. A period where there is *more* code running than usual, or *less*.

If you want there to be no visible downtime with a deployment, the likely case if you are practicing continuous deployment, then you will be experiencing the state where there is more code than usual running. The duration of this will vary with the strategy used to bring the new version online. Even in the simplest case, where the old version is disabled as soon as the new one is running, there is a period of time where both are active which must be accounted for. There are more complex strategies for incremental activation of new code. In all cases, they result in a longer period of overlap.

The other choice is taking downtime to deploy. Stop the old code, start the new. The system is unavailable for a period of time while the deployment is occurring. From a user perspective, or the perspective of a collaborating service, this is no different than an unplanned failure. While this isn't providing resiliency for the code that is being deployed, in a system composed of multiple services, being able to individually deploy a service and having its collaborators handle it being available is resiliency in action.

Whether the starting point is in handling unexpected failures, or smoothing a deployment process, they are complementary and support each other. Being able to handle failure uniformly across the system aids in management and remediation.

Elastic

Elasticity is the trickiest to utilize, and it's also the hardest to align a clear benefit. Effective utilization is an advanced topic. I believe the important part is making it *possible*, because adding elasticity to a system that hadn't accounting for these extension points can be a challenge.

If a system experiences a constant usage level, there's no elasticity in the workload. If there is variability in the usage level, it must be a significant enough variation to warrant allocating or releasing system resources. Our business applications are more likely to be measured in requests per minute, a doubling of which may not be a significant change. Given a cloud environment where there is a three-instance cluster for resiliency, effectively auto-scaling this size of cluster is tricky. It may be better to increase to a new fixed size rather than the spending time fine-tuning an auto-scaling policy. If you have a large cluster, auto-scaling is easier.

However, on the flip side, if the variability is significant and auto-scaling can be effective, being elastic saves costs. It will longer be necessary to over-provision resources to handle peak loads, removing the need to pay for unused capacity during the quieter periods. If cost is already a factor, a system may be intentionally under-provisioned relative to peak loads with a reliance on luck, hoping that the peaks don't lead to too many undesirable outcomes.

Message Driven

This is the ultimate answer. To a degree, the other properties represent "nice to haves" in a business application. The primary benefit in building a business application is a reactive system is to be message driven.

The prior three properties, responsive, resilient, and elastic, can be seen as operational. To be truly message driven, the system's architecture needs to operate in that manner into its core. This property fundamentally effects system architecture. As I discussed in the prior chapter, your system is already composed of messages. Our goal is to preserve them.

Let's think about the types of messages that exist in a system, their purposes, and the value in retaining the abstraction.

Imagine a status-quo service, a colloquial REST endpoint storing data in a relational database via an ORM. A HTTP request to change some data in the system is a message. The request is consumed by the application, and using the appropriate logic, updates the object model and persists the changes. A response message is returned.

We started with a message, the request, and end with a message, the response. We have *transformed* the request into the response.

Breaking this example down further, the HTTP request is a message representing a *request for change* to the system. Conceptually, this is a **command**. There is often some validation on the incoming request to ensure that it is structurally sound, such as checking for required fields. If those have succeeded, we can consider the command to have been *accepted* by the application.

The application consumes this command and updates the object model. This is likely still prospective, as there may be database constraints that need to be met. It isn't until transaction commit time that the application knows for certain that the update has been a success. This is the *processing* of the command. The transaction disposition, whether it committed successfully or failed, is the command's *result*.

If the result is a failure, an error response can be immediately returned, a transformation of the result. In success case, the object model that was modified as part of the command is probably used to return a response payload, another type of transformation. Each case, success or failure, represents another message.

Without an explicit representation of the command, it is easy for the above logic to become conflated, making testing more difficult. This can go against the developer's expectation of the system, being amenable to change. The inherit structure of the application requires constant vigilance to prevent this.

If we reify the command as a message, we can operate upon it explicitly. There is a straightforward processing pipeline for this command. Each step can be represented by a discrete, testable, piece of code. Ultimately, that is what this book is about, and Part 3 is an in-depth exploration of how to achieve this.

By using an explicit command, the system can be message driven. In utilizing this representation of what the system is doing, it provides a framework for how its logical components interact. This consistent (and yes, opinionated) design philosophy informs how the application is structured.

Exchanging messages between components allows us to apply the same inversion of control that is used in wiring up component references to the system's data flow. The same benefits are reaped, improved reuse, reducing coupling, and independent evolution.

In a business application, where it is acting as a source of truth and managing workflows, it is paramount to be able to change how the data flows safely and with confidence. That is the reason to build them as a reactive system.

Summary

This chapter has explained *why* it is beneficial to build business applications as reactive systems. The business has expectations on the application's reliability that are provided by a reactive system. The most important is your expectation of being able to effectively change the system. In modeling the application's data flow as messages, this can be done with confidence. Part 3 will explain *how*. Before that, the next two chapters go further in depth with two important features of business applications, managing business rules, and time.

CHAPTER 5

What Is a Business Rule?

A business application is a source of truth for the business. In order to be effective at this task, data will need to conform to a structure. This will allow processes and workflows to be built around it. Categorically, the specification of a data's structure, how it is modified, and what happens when it is changed are all considered **business rules**. At a given point in time, they will be specific. As the business changes, so will its rules. This chapter explores how I think about rules and how to classify them. By understanding their relationship to the system, we will know where to place them in our architecture.

Thinking About Business Rules

Having the correct rules is critical. Having the wrong rules leads to users working outside of the system, around its constraints. As one of the main goals of the business is to have users actually *use* the system, the rules need to accurately reflect how the business conducts itself, inclusive of exceptions.

What are the correct rules though? Someone must speak to prospective users to understand. This may be a part of your responsibilities, or in a larger organization, this may be part of a Product Manager's duties. Understanding business rules are a critical part of gathering requirements.

It is important to gather requirements from the correct audience. If only management is interviewed, there may be a disconnect between how they think work happens, and how the business *actually* conducts itself. It is important to be aware of this disconnect. The field of human factors and ergonomics describes this as Work-as-Imagined vs. Work-as-Done. In creating an application, we are encoding a third form, Work-as-Prescribed. If your organization does incident analysis and retrospectives, you may have been exposed to these concepts. The burgeoning discipline of Site Reliability Engineering, a practice that applies software engineering principles to operations, has been using these concepts when conducting blameless postmortems for failures.

© Peter Royal 2023
P. Royal, *Building Modern Business Applications*, https://doi.org/10.1007/978-1-4842-8992-1_5

As an application developer, we control what is possible to do with the application. We are prescribing how work must be performed within the context of our system. The act of gathering requirements is the process of understanding how work should be done, as imagined, and formalizing those processes in the system. A developer's pedantic accuracy can be a benefit in this process, asking the necessary questions to understand possible edge cases.

When determining your system's rules, it is important to remember that there is an element of risk as part of their formalization. In adding a constraint that must be true, it removes the possibility of data that would violate it. This represents a form of risk. If the business needs to change that decision, how quickly could a change be safely made? Being amenable to this type of change is one of our goals.

There is a difference between different in something that must be always true, and something that should probably be true. One is a rule, the other is a guideline. Keep this in mind as we discuss how to categorize rules.

Categorizations

Over my career, I've observed common themes in what's called a "business rule" and have used those themes to construct the following categorizations.

Data at Rest

Ultimately, data is stored *somewhere*. There will be requirements that this data must meet.

If you've created a table in a relational database, you've encountered rules for data at rest. Any constraint that is expressed in a database's schema falls into this category. These include nullability, uniqueness, and foreign keys. Some databases allow the expression of more complex constraints for a column, such as defining a fixed range for a numerical value, or even across columns in a table, such as a "start date" must be before an "end date." In SQL, these are CHECK constraints.

These declarative constraints are constrained to a single row, which limits what they can enforce. Imagine a system that is tracking widgets. If there is a table that represents the available inventory of widgets there may be the requirement that the sum across all rows can't go below zero. If each row represents an operation that adds or removes a widget, the table may have a constraint such as CHECK (count <> 0) to ensure that each row has a nonzero count, as a valid operation must move some quantity of widgets. To express that the inventory can never be negative, it may seem straightforward to write CHECK (SUM(count) >= 0). Alas, I'm not aware of any widely used relational database that allows specification of this type of constraint in a declarative fashion. Constraints are only checked in the context of a single row, not an entire table. Table-wise or cross-table constraints require the use of a trigger to invoke procedural code stored in the database.

This jump from a declarative to procedural constraint means that these constraints are generally implemented outside the database. As test-driven development, and more broadly unit testing and continuous integration have become more popular, the ability to automate testing has been more valuable to developers. Procedural logic within a database is harder to test, as it requires a running instance of the database software. Until the popularization of Docker in the mid-to-late 2010s, the effort to achieve this was generally unfeasible for most teams, time was better spent elsewhere. For the JVM, there are a handful of embedded database engines that can be used for tests, but they do have differences compared to the ones that must be used in production. It has pushed developers to rely on the lowest common denominator of database features in their code.

If a constraint is only enforced in application code, there's the philosophical and practical question of whether it is actually always true. In order to guarantee that a constraint for data at rest is enforced, all modifications to the data must go through the enforcement mechanism. If that isn't within the data store itself, access to the data store must be carefully guarded to prevent modifications that bypass the application and interact with the store directly.

Enforcing constraints in application code does allow for easier management of changing constraints over time. If a constraint is weakened, there's no change needed for existing data, it already meets the looser constraint. If a constraint is tightened, such as making an optional field required, a decision must be made for existing data that would be in violation of the new constraint. This may be a consideration in enforcing a constraint in application code rather than the database. The next chapter will explore time and its relationship to business rules in greater depth.

Another form of the *data at rest* rule is a workflow with progressive statuses. Consider an entity that is passing through a workflow where there may be different requirements upon its data for it to move to the next step. Imagine a system that allows placing an order for a custom bicycle. To start an order, there isn't any required information. You've started the process, made a few selections, but then want to save it for later. The application may offer that as part of its workflow, saving your progress. In order to save an order for later there is additional required information, your e-mail address. There are five decision points in the customization process, and you can make a choice on any number while continuing to repeatedly save the order for later. In order to proceed to the "ready to order" status though, a choice is required on each one of those five decision points. As the bicycle order entity moves through the workflow, there are progressive requirements for completeness of the data.

There is a subtle distinction in the workflow example, the separation of the requirements of the state to be at the next "ready for" status vs. completing what the next state of the workflow may represent. Our bicycle order workflow may distinguish between "ready to submit" and "submitted." In workflows, there are often coordination points with external systems, side effects.

Side Effects

Applications are generally not acting in isolation. Our business applications will nearly always interact with the business. In acting as a source of truth and automating workflows, changes to the data within the system will initiate other activities. Collectively, I'm calling this class of activities *side effects*.

This term is borrowed from computer science, where it refers to functions that modify state outside of their local environment. Consider the following function:

```
private int multiply(int a, int b) {
    var result = a * b;
    System.out.println(a + " * " + b + " = " + result);
    return result;
}
```

Printing to the console is a side effect. Mapping this example to a larger application, our system is equivalent to the function, and interactions with other systems are side effects.

These are tasks that happen *after* data has changed. You'll recognize them in application requirements, as they generally take the form of:

```
if/when <precondition> then <do something>
```

Concretely, they may do things like:

- Send users a welcome email after signing up

- After an order is created, send information to another system for fulfillment

- After a payment is approved, send it to the bank

Interaction with another system *before* changing data in your system is not a side effect, it's a part of a workflow. This distinction matters because it isn't necessarily the responsibility of your system to perform that interaction. As a matter of practical implementation, it may, be there would be no change to the overall behavior of the workflow if it happened elsewhere. A workflow may, and likely will, span multiple applications. When considering rules *for your application*, it is only the side effects that it needs to initiate that are in consideration here.

When implementing a system, it is important to separate side effects from the modification of data that makes the precondition true. It may seem like a straightforward implementation, but the failure modes are undesirable. If you update an order's payment status to approved and send it to the bank before ensuring the updated status has been successfully written to your database, what happens if the database update fails?

My ideal implementation of side effects is by modeling them as a state machine. Your application may be a part of a larger business workflow, also ideally modeled as a state machine that spans multiple applications. Similar to how reactive systems compose, so do state machines. The same underlying pattern can be used for each side effect, and the value comes down to how failure is managed. By using a state machine, the application can track its attempts at successfully performing the side effect, allowing for appropriate error handling.

The state machine should explicitly track the start of an attempt to perform a side effect. If a failure occurs while performing it, the next step is likely different than a mere repetition of the initial action. If we start to send a payment but experience a failure in the middle of the process, retrying may not be the appropriate action. Using the example of sending a payment after an order's approval again, if sending the payment fails, the next action will depend upon the behavior of the system we are sending the payment to. If the receiving system is idempotent, the original action can be retried. Rather than a "success" response, we may receive a "failure" that represents "already processed," indicating that our initial attempt was in fact successful, even though we saw it as a failure. Receiving "already processed" on the first attempt would be unexpected and an error state. If the receiving system weren't idempotent, a different mechanism would need to be used to determine what the next step should be.

Actions performed as side effects should be idempotent whenever possible. In practice, this can be done by requiring callers to provide a unique identifier per invocation, allowing receivers to identify duplicate requests.

Derivable Data

All the data within an application is not equal. Continuing the example from the earlier section, the total count of widgets must always be greater than or equal to zero. The value that a business rule is checking is often also displayed to users in some fashion. In this example, it's the "available widgets."

A straightforward implementation would be to recalculate the total when necessary, persist the total, and use the persisted value within the user interface. This is a valid approach that would meet the needs of the business.

Embedded in this example are conflated concerns which should be thought about independently, even if the implementation does tie them together. There are two business rules here:

1. A constraint on the *operations*, that their aggregate must satisfy.

2. Usage of the aggregate for display in the user interface.

The distinction may be subtle, but I believe it is important. The constraint around the total is not a constraint on the total as an independent piece of data. When adding a new operation, and needing to ensure that the first rule is met, how do you think about the operation? Is it

- Add the operation, recalculate/update the total, and check that it satisfies the constraint?

Or,

- Take the prior total, check that the addition of the new operation would not cause the constraint to be violated, and then add the operation?

In the former, the operation is added without concern for the constraint check, treating the derived total as the data that the constraint is placed upon. In the latter, the check is on the new operation, using the prior total as an optimization, rather than recomputing it each time.

While the first rule is a constraint on the aggregate value, it does not mean that the aggregate value must be stored. That's the essence of the distinction. The aggregate is an example of a *derived value*.

When building a data model for a system, it is important to separate out the most fundamental facts that underly the model, and the derivative facts that build upon them.

Relative to constraints on data at rest, the mention of a derived value can be thought of as an "extracted variable," and a means to speak about the derivation without repeating what it is derived from each time. If the derived value is *only* used in constraints for data at rest, it doesn't really exist as a data point in the system.

If the derived value is *also* used for display purposes, the act of deriving it is what I consider to be *display logic*. This is the third classification of business rules. Display logic is a **nondestructive** transformation of a system's data. The nondestructive aspect is critical. In mathematical terms, the logic should be a *pure function*, returning the same result given the same inputs.

If display logic obeys this property, acting as a nondestructive transformation of data, it is not a requirement to store the result. Given the inputs and the version of code that backs the transformation, an identical result can be achieved. Storage of the derived value is an optimization, rather than a requirement.

Another variation of display logic is the usage of information from another system. Sometimes, this will be very straightforward, displaying data from another system as-is. Other times, there will be a transformation of data from your system that uses data from another system as one of its inputs. In financial systems, currency conversions are a good example of this. There may be another system that provides exchange rates, and the act of displaying data from your system in another currency using an exchange rate from another system is another form of display logic.

In naming something "display logic," it is not meant to imply that the logic exists within our application's user interface code. For performance reasons, an application may persist the output of display logic. This should be thought of as a cache on the results, rather than the fundamental facts of the system. If that analogy does not hold in your use-case, I would question whether it is display logic, or if it should be considered a fundamental fact.

Summary

These categorizations of business rules inform how to think about the properties of your application's model. This book does not describe how to go about defining your model. Rather, I am focusing on how to approach its implementation. An implementation provides some amount of feedback into a design. My hope here is that thinking of your business rules according to these categories will help clarify your design.

Business rules can fall into one of the following categories:

- Constraints for data at rest

- Side effects, such as process initiation, when data changes

- Display logic, including derivation and aggregation

These categories describe the relationship of the rule to the data within the system. This will be useful later, as it can inform where in our design the implementation should be placed. We will get to that in the third part of this book. Before that, there is one last prerequisite, the management of time. It has a critical interaction with business rules, as rules change over time, and their relationship with data needs to reflect that.

CHAPTER 6

Managing Time

Can time be "managed"? In our applications, we have control over their communication, and through that manage how they learn about, communicate, and process data. It is through this, controlling the flow of information, that time itself is managed. When we create business applications, we are establishing a virtual microcosm of the business itself. As a source of truth, the timeline that the application creates can be an official timeline for the question of "what happened?".

Answering "What Happened?"

A common question I've had from users of business applications I've worked on has been "why does the system have this value?". The value may have been the result of a calculation, data received from another system, or provided by a user. In all of these situations, the system needs to *remember* its inputs in order to answer the question.

The simplest example is a business rule for derived data, as I discussed in the prior chapter. The inputs to the rule are stored in the system, and the derived value is used as a part of display logic. It is then straightforward to augment a calculation to have its output also contain a copy of its inputs. This will allow an observer that understands the rule to independently verify the calculation.

Beyond that simple example, things are more difficult. If a calculation result is persisted, how do we know what its inputs were at the time of calculation? Ideally, they would have been recorded, but was that an explicit product requirement? If not, it likely wasn't done. If the persistence of the value included a timestamp, you could try and reconstruct what the data was at that time.

In order to answer the question, we need to know what the data in the system was at a *prior point in time*. If the system isn't tracking that at the time it occurred, the information will ultimately be lost. This is the "mutate in place" of a status-quo architecture.

47

P. Royal, *Building Modern Business Applications*, https://doi.org/10.1007/978-1-4842-8992-1_6

Tracking Changes

In our status-quo architectures, there are two patterns to tracking changes that you may be familiar with. Each has varying levels of complexity.

If tracking changes is primarily for use by those supporting the application, it may utilize a history table. Given a table to track customers:

```
CREATE TABLE customers (
    customer_id   BIGINT PRIMARY KEY,
    customer_name TEXT
);
```

The following history table may be employed:

```
CREATE TABLE customer_history (
    -- 0/1/2, indicating insert/update/delete
    revision_type      INT,
    revision_timestamp TIMESTAMP,
    customer_id        BIGINT,
    customer_name      TEXT
);
```

Here, `revision_type` is an enumeration indicating the type of change (insert, update or delete) and `revision_timestamp` is when the change was recorded. There will be a design decision of whether this is the row from `customers` before or after the change.

If change tracking is an application feature, the complexity of conditionally querying a history table may be undesirable. Instead, all values over time may be captured in the same table:

```
CREATE TABLE customers (
    valid_from    TIMESTAMP,
    valid_to      TIMESTAMP,
    customer_id   BIGINT,
    customer_name TEXT
);
```

In this example, `valid_from` and `valid_to` capture two points in time that indicate when the row was valid. This model can easily support point-in-time queries asking, "what was the customer's name as of a specific time." There is additional complexity at write time, as the new value needs to be inserted and the valid_to timestamp for the prior record needs to be adjusted. This model also breaks easily using customer_id as a primary key, as there will be multiple rows with the value. A more complex constraint is required, one that can ensure that there's only a single value for a primary key at a given timestamp.

There is an additional pitfall in each of these approaches. The database schema is *unified across time*. The only safe changes possible are the relaxing of constraints, making a NON NULL column allow NULL, or to add a new nullable column. Any other type of change either risks changing existing data or will require changing data.

This presents a dilemma. Is the past not to be preserved as it was, or will the application need to adjust in other ways? Any solution will have drawbacks and will result in "tech debt." This is a system that isn't amenable to change.

Even if one of the two prior, or perhaps an alternate, approach is taken, a problem still remains, capturing *why*.

Why Did That Happen?

By storing prior values, we can see what that past was. By comparing past states, we can see how values have changed. This is sufficient to answer *what*. However, I've found that the real question that users have is *why*.

Data doesn't change in a vacuum. There is a cause-and-effect interaction. The change tracking mechanisms I mentioned are only capturing the effect, the "what." The data model itself isn't set up to capture the cause, the "why."

The "why" may be inferable. If you know what operations were possible in the application at the time the change was made, you can use that knowledge to pattern match against the data to see if it was made with a given operation. This would be dependent upon having specific code paths for each change type, which may not be in place if the application is using the "colloquial REST" from Chapter 2. If the user interface interacts by sending a payload with updated state, that context will have been lost.

I hope there is some familiarity with the nature of this problem. It is one that we, as developers, have encountered and solved for ourselves. We experience this with our source code and have solved it with version control (VCS). This is a best practice, for good reason. In its basic form, a VCS system tracks the changes to a codebase, the "what." When a change is made, you have the option of providing a message, the "why." There's no requirement that a reasonable message is provided. I've worked with developers that have treated it like a bothersome gatekeeper, providing a token message to satisfy the requirement. I've impressed the notion that a good commit message *explains why* the change was made. The "what" is obvious, it is the change itself. While I may remember why tomorrow, I may not a year from now. I've described commit messages as "notes to my future self." Even when working solo, I make them meaningful.

If it is a best practice to track all changes to a system's code, why isn't it also a best practice to track all changes to a system's data? I believe the answer is **it should be**. I believe that in the past this was infeasible. Tracking all changes to data will require an ever-increasing storage capacity. Today, the capacities of modern storage systems, especially combined with on-demand cloud-based storage, make this entirely practical. How may a system that stores changes be conceptualized?

Events

When we think about storing changes, they are events: an outcome or result from an operation that has happened in a system. With this view, every change is an event. By storing events, we can construct a canonical timeline of changes to a system. A time-ordered collection of events is a log, or ledger. This is how VCS systems operate conceptually, as they expose a history of changes to us.

In a business application, an event should be the changes to the data as well as the *intent* of the change. This is capturing both *what* and *why*. A log of events is useful to describe the past, but it is inefficient to understand the present. Having to traverse an ever-growing event log to find pieces of data doesn't scale. Instead, we can keep a running result of what all the events imply and use that to answer questions about the present. In a VCS, that's your "checkout" of a repository onto a filesystem. The act of using events to construct a "state of the world" at a given point in time is *materialization*.

This technique is known as *event sourcing*; storing changes to the system as events and constructing materializations of those events to answer questions. By representing changes as events, they become messages. This brings us back to the reactive manifesto; representing changes to a systems data as events allow the changes to be messages.

We can also apply the same technique to a *request to change* the system's data.

Commands

Commands and events are two sides to the same coin. Their difference lies in their relationship to the data in the system. A continuously updated materialization of all of a system's events is the *current state* of the system.

Events are backward looking. They describe what has happened. Commands are forward looking. They describe a *request to change* the system of the system. A key word is *request*. The desire to make a change doesn't mean that it will be permitted. It may or may not be, depending upon the business rules for data at rest.

This is a concept from a pattern known as Command Query Responsibility Segregation (CQRS). With that pattern, there is a model that state changes operate upon, and a separate model for querying. There is a natural complementation with event sourcing. Events can be materialized in multiple ways, one to service queries, and another for enforcing business rules for data at rest. I refer to the latter as *command processing*. It is the act of taking a command and determining if it is allowed, and if so, what events it implies.

I want to point out that this *is not novel*. These ideas and patterns have been floating around and in practice for decades. I do believe that the *practicality* or *applicability* has changed in recent years. These are valuable practices for business applications, and are suitable for forward-looking, modern, architectures.

Understanding Time

I started this chapter from the historical perspective, how to answer the question "What happened?". That led to introducing events as a fine-grained way of memorializing both *what* and *why*. Commands are the precursors for events, and events can be used to construct a notion of state. These concepts map cleanly to time. Commands represent the future, events are the past, and state is the present.

This allows us to construct a localized timeline within a system. It is possible to time travel to the past by only materializing a portion of the events. This is a *local* timeline though. Let's digress and explore *what time represents*.

Time is a means of communicating *when*. Communication requires a common reference. Here on Earth, we use Coordinated Universal Time (UTC).

When receiving communication as to when something, and event, occurred, there are two dimensions of interest:

1. The time that the event *occurred*.

2. The time that you became *aware* of the event having occurred.

Each of these is a discrete point in time. **They are always different!** Sometimes, the difference is negligible, such as actions that you perform, but not always.

If you touch a stove, your finger will burn before you're aware that the stove is hot. This is a visceral example of the propagation delay of information. The time between 1 and 2, although short, is long enough to burn your hand. You need to be *aware* of an event and take action upon it. It is only when you are aware of the temperature of the stove that you can move your hand.

In many systems, these two dimensions are conflated. The time that the system receives information ends up being the canonical time for when the event occurred. It is important to understand that this is a fiction and will result in disparities if a system has multiple sources of truth.

Serialization of Time

Ultimately an application will generate a single timeline of "what happened." In many applications, this is not explicitly managed, and it is delegated to the relational database that is storing data. It is then up to the transaction isolation level to control how time flows. There is only one mode that provides full consistency, SERIALIZABLE. It is not the default for any major relational database. I suspect that is partially due to performance, and partially due to the onus it places on application developers.

The default settings for most databases allow developers to operate with the database in a way that generally results in no errors. They will be sufficiently rare such that an error can be propagated far out into the call stack, perhaps resulting in the need for a user to retry an operation.

SERIALIZABLE is different. It requires all interactions to be strictly linearizable. If that would be violated by a modification, an error is returned, and the transaction must be retried. This requires application developers to have structured their code that interacts with the database to support multiple invocations. If the types of business rules are intermixed, such as performing side effects, there is a risk of performing the side effects multiple times.

Ultimately, the database's transaction log is an ordered list of changes that have been made. It is an *event log*, tucked away inside of the database.

By representing requests for changes as commands and storing them as events, we hoist this event log into our application, allowing the system to use it as a first-class construct. This allows *us* to control the serialization of time. In deciding the order of commands to process, we are building a timeline.

Eventual Consistency

A serialization of time provides local consistency. However, our applications aren't operating in a vacuum. They are *a* source of truth for the business, but not *the* source of all truths. Eventual consistency is referring to the propagation of information over time. As system B becomes aware of changes in system A, B is *eventually consistent* with A.

There is no one true timeline. In a large system composed of many applications, each application will have its own perspective on the order that events happened, as each will become aware of events independently.

Generally, this may be acceptable. By using events to communicate what happened, each application can keep track of when it became aware of information, allowing local answers to "what happened." However, in business applications, sometimes when an event occurred is also important, and that must be tracked as well.

Bitemporality

Bitemporality is tracking *both* of our time dimensions, when an event occurred, and when the system became aware of it. In the business domain, an example of this would be a retroactive policy.

Imagine a loyalty program where points are awarded for purchases. Points are a form of currency and can be spent with the business. Unspent points expire after a period of time. In our example, points expire a year after they are earned.

The point tracking application is a separate application. It consumes transaction events from elsewhere in the business to track its state of point balances and directly manages transactions for spending points. Due to this, it has two points of time it tracks, when it is aware of transactions, as well as when the transaction occurred. It is bitemporal.

My point balance "today" is subject to how up to date the application is with the transaction event stream. Points are awarded based on the date the transaction occurred, not when it was seen by the point tracking application.

For any past point in time there are two views of the point balance. What was the point balance based on the information that was known *at the time*, and what was the point balance based on what is known *now*.

An event log that keeps two timestamps makes answering each of these straightforward, a transaction time, and a received time. To answer what the balance was based on what was known at the time, only events with a received time prior to the time in question would be consulted. To answer what the past balance was based on all available information, transaction time would be used.

In this hypothetical system, transaction time may be the primary timestamp used. However, there is still value in recording received time. If a loyalty program customer has a question about their point balance, having information about received time can be invaluable in answering questions. Data is valuable, and it is best to capture it when possible.

In addition to this contrived example, there is a generally applicable form of bitemporality, changing business rules.

Business Rule Changes

I've mentioned *amenability to change* as an important property of a business application. Business will change, and the speed with which their software can adapt can be a gating factor.

The flow of events can be seen as the flow of time. As events occur, time passes. Events don't have to be confined to changes in *data*, they can also represent changes to *behavior*.

Reusing the example of a loyalty program, imagine it in the context of an airline. There may be a situation, such as a global pandemic, where the airline wishes to extend the expiration of all points by a year. That is, if you had points that were due to expire within a given period of time, that expiration is extended by a year. Any points accrued during the next year should have a two-year expiration window. How should this be modeled?

One way is to use an *event* to represent the rule change. When the application is materializing events, it would use a rule change event as a marker to adjust its behavior. By incorporating business rule changes into the event log, it enriches the event log as a source-of-truth.

The implementation of this idea can vary, the event can be very specific, invoking a targeted code in a materialization process, or it could contain parameters if this rule is something that is frequently adjusted (if it were done for brief promotional periods).

By taking *control of time*, we have the opportunity to do richer things inside of our application. It also enables more in-depth answers to "what happened" and "why," as both the data and the rules are available for introspection.

Summary

We have covered

- Tracking data changes over time.

- What are events and commands

- The difference between the time an event occurred and when our system is aware of it having occurred

- Managing business rule changes over time

This concludes the second part. I've discussed reactive systems, business rules, and time. These are concepts that I find important to understand before proposing a design for a business application. The next part will use these concepts to build a design, and ultimately an implementation.

PART III

Design

CHAPTER 7

Constraints and Principles

It's design time! The first two parts of this book were context setting. I needed to ensure that we had a shared understanding of a business application as well as an understanding of common patterns in use today. I then introduced reactive systems via the Reactive Manifesto and my rationale for why to build a business application as a reactive system. Finally, I described my categorizations of business rules and how time is an important (and sometimes underappreciated) dimension.

This part of the book will work toward my proposed design for business applications. The first step in that path will be to introduce some self-imposed constraints on the design as well as self-selected guiding principles that will inform the architecture. Let's dive in.

Constraints

There are two constraints I want to impose on the design, and they are both around how the application presents itself to the UI. I'm going to briefly mention them and then explain them in more detail.

The first is to enable and encourage the UI to be built in a manner that supports real-time updates of data. The second is to use GraphQL to drive the UI experience.

From REST to a Graph

I briefly mentioned GraphQL in Chapter 2, and it deserves a comprehensive description. Let's step back and think of what led up to it as a way of explaining why I believe it to be an important technology.

It is possible to view the data inside of a system as a giant graph. The hierarchical path portion of a URL has been used as a way to index into that conceptual graph. This was the basis for architecting data APIs. An endpoint such as /api/v3/customers would list customers. To access a specific customer, the key would be appended as another

59

P. Royal, *Building Modern Business Applications*, https://doi.org/10.1007/978-1-4842-8992-1_7

path segment, `/api/v3/customers/42`. Customers have multiple addresses, and those could be enumerated at `/api/v3/customers/42/addresses`. A specific address could then be accessed at `/api/v3/customers/42/addresses/67`.

This hierarchical indexing into the data graph has two drawbacks:

1. Traversal requires multiple requests.

2. No straightforward mechanism to indicate what data is desired in each request.

At the scale of our business applications, these drawbacks generally aren't an impediment. However, for two Silicon Valley companies, Facebook and Netflix, these drawbacks were enough to have them contemporaneously develop alternative approaches. They each build upon this idea of using the path hierarchy and the data at each path to form a unified graph of a system's data. I'll discuss Netflix's solution first.

Falcor

Netflix developed a technology named Falcor.[1] It views the unified data graph as a single JSON document, with a mechanism for allowing the hierarchical nature of JSON to have cycles and thus model a graph. Callers would then provide a "path" (similar to, but not the same syntax as, JSONPath) to indicate which portions of the graph to load. This allows UIs to fetch *precisely* what they need in a single request. Netflix's model is a clear evolution from hierarchical paths that return JSON fragments, as it collapses everything into a single endpoint allowing UIs to specify paths that go beyond what the URL paths provided and into the JSON payloads.

GraphQL

Facebook took a slightly different approach with GraphQL. It also builds upon the notion that the system is a giant graph. GraphQL has a schema to describe the graph. Graph nodes are object types, and each type is composed of fields. A critical differentiator is that fields in GraphQL can accept arguments. Rather than a graph of pure data, GraphQL should be viewed as a graph of *functions*. Just as one could pass query parameters to REST endpoints, the same can be done with fields on a GraphQL type.

---

[1] `https://github.com/Netflix/falcor`

Unlike Falcor, GraphQL doesn't impose the perspective that the graph is a single conceptual JSON document. While Falcor uses the document abstraction as a mechanism to provide a "root" of the graph for its path-based access, GraphQL has a special type in the graph, the Query type, whose fields define entry points into the graph.

The graph-of-functions abstraction also allows GraphQL to have a solution for data modifications, another REST behavior that it preserves. Modifications, or mutations in its terminology, are performed by requesting the fields of another special type, the Mutation type.

Although both Falcor and GraphQL were released within a month of each other in 2015, GraphQL has had far more success. I believe this is due to it having a complete answer for replacing REST-style access patterns.

Why GraphQL

GraphQL sits in a position similar to that of SQL. It defines a data model and how to interact with it, but at its core doesn't prescribe anything else. Its specification[2] focuses on how a schema can be defined and the execution model that should be used in order to satisfy queries. There are conventions and libraries to enable exposing a service over HTTP, but the underlying abstractness of the specification would allow for alternate transports.

In defining a schema, and by encouraging users of GraphQL to start with defining a schema, GraphQL services are self-documenting. GraphQL requires clients to specify *exactly* the data they wish to retrieve, there's no facility for wildcarding the fields of a type. This allows the usage of each field to be tracked. When combined with the built-in deprecation facility, the necessary elements to allow for schema evolution are present.

For building user interfaces, which is a goal of a business application, there are many tools available for interacting with GraphQL services. As of my writing of this book, React is the zeitgeist for creating web UIs, and its ecosystem is heavily influenced by GraphQL. Should trends change, GraphQL would still be appropriate.

---

[2]https://spec.graphql.org/

Being Real-Time

I believe that business applications should have the same real-time capabilities as consumer applications. I touched on this in Chapter 2 when mentioning the status quo. XMLHTTPRequest made it possible to load data without a page refresh, but it retains the request/response paradigm. There are two additional web technologies that allow for data to be streamed to the browser, Server Sent Events (SSE), which is a push-only mechanism, and WebSockets, which allows for a bidirectional push-based channel. These two technologies are now widely deployed and available for use. However, effective use requires a system whose architecture is amenable for this type of real-time interaction.

This is another reason to use GraphQL. GraphQL has a third special type, the Subscription type. A Subscription field returns a *stream* of values. When combined with a streaming transport such as SSE or WebSockets, GraphQL can act as a single solution for queries, mutations, and real-time updates.

Principles

Before embarking upon a project, I like to have an articulable set of principles that development will follow. In stating a set of principles, it helps provide guidance to your teammates and whoever may be responsible for future maintenance of the system. As principles, they are values that will be strived for. Unlike constraints, they are guidance, rather than a requirement. I will first enumerate the set, and then discuss each in turn:

- Never Forget

- Message Driven

- Read/Write Separation

- Partial Availability

- Design Flexibility

- Modularity

- Testability

- Amenability to Change

Never Forget

The phrasing of this is from a floppy disk company that was around when I was growing up, Elephant Memory Systems. Their logo was an elephant's face and underneath it said, "Never Forgets." This was a homage to the idiom "an elephant never forgets", and that phrasing has stuck with me.

As I discussed in the last chapter around time, there are techniques that can be used to have a system retain prior states. It is a best practice for developers to record all code changes in a version control system. It should also be a best practice to architect business applications similarly. The data contained within a business application can be critical to the success of the business, and the default policy should be to track any changes.

"Never Forget" goes a step further, as it isn't the simple mechanics of recording the new state, it is recording the intention behind the change, remembering the "what" and the "why."

As a principle, I believe this is something to add at the start of a project. Unless changes are captured as they happen, the information will be forever lost.

Message Driven

This principle is taken directly from the Reactive Manifesto. I discussed the basics of this in the third chapter when introducing reactive systems. Again, this principle is one that is best adhered to at the start of the project. Retrofitting a message passing onto a system that was not designed for this type of communication can be challenging. By being message driven from the start, the system is set up to make use of the other properties from the manifesto, elasticity, resiliency, and responsiveness.

There is a critical control aspect here. By reifying internal communication in our system as messages, we gain control over them. Messages become discrete items that can be manipulated by our code. Message passing is one of the original ideas behind "object-oriented programming" (OOP). Developers aren't often aware of this, as it is often the encapsulation that objects provide that is more prominently featured.

We want to reuse the ideas of encapsulation and message passing in our system. The components that exchange messages will be more coarse-grained than an object-oriented domain model. We will need to have facilities for message passing on top of what our implementation language provides. Not all languages allow for dynamic handling of messages between objects, Ruby and Objective-C being two notable ones that do. Even if we were using one of those languages to implement our system, we will want to have a mechanism on top of the language facilities to manipulate the message flow.

Read/Write Separation

The read-and-write access patterns for a system are often not symmetric. For young systems with a small user base, this generally poses no problems. Few users and a short lifespan mean the data volume and change rates will be lower.

As a system matures, the data contained within often increases with its time in service. In our proposed system, this will be exacerbated as we will be storing prior states as well.

Our business applications will be serving two purposes for the business, data entry and decision support. Data entry access patterns often require the ability to "read your writes." A user that has made a change to the system is acutely aware of what the application should now show them, they expect reads to be consistent with the writes they have performed. Classically, this type of activity is known as Online Transaction Processing (OLTP).

Decision support is different. Users of a system for this use-case are often not making changes to the data. They're running reports and asking complex aggregation questions of the application. As they aren't making changes, the users won't notice if the data is slightly out of date. The questions that are being asked may also be completely tolerant to out-of-date data, as they're always looking back a fixed period of time. Think of a daily report that's run, as long as the data is up to date by the report's execution time, the report's requirements are met. This type of activity is known as Online Analytical Processing (OLAP).

In larger businesses, OLAP activity is often performed across systems that departments or other subdivisions of the business use. A system's data will be replicated to a central store that aggregates information from other systems.

The users of your system may have some similar requirements, and I've found this to be a common request: in-app analytics and reporting.

When using a relational database, a natural solution to this can be to add a read replica of the database and use it to satisfy these types of requests. However, a system that was not designed with that in mind may have challenges introducing another database host and using it appropriately.

Thus, this principle is a means to side-step those future problems by addressing them early. If the system is designed with separate paths for reads and writes, the system is amenable to change in this dimension. An initial implementation may very well use a single database instance for everything. By introducing the logical separation earlier, if and when there's a need for a physical separation, the changes to the system will be easier to make.

Partial Availability

Our business applications are important to the business, that's why they've invested in them! They need to be available *when the business requires it*. Historically, prior to widerspread Internet adoption, the usage of business software was often tied to business hours. While some domains have been operating around-the-clock for years, others have had the relative luxury of usage being tied to local business hours.

Having a regular period of inactivity for a system creates a natural window to perform maintenance activities. With such opportunities, it's possible to take a system completely offline to do the work. As applications start to have components that have outward-facing components such as user interfaces for the business's customers, or an API integration with customer or vendor systems, taking an application completely out of service becomes harder and harder.

As a principle, partial availability is the ability to take only a *portion* of the system down for maintenance or upgrades. It's also the ability to only have a portion *fail*. This is a form of resiliency, one of the desired Reactive Manifesto properties.

The granularity of what is partially available will depend upon your business domain, and the nature of the application. There are cross-cutting coarse facets, such as being available for reads, but not for writes. Domain-specific facets will require coordination with the business to under what the "blast radius" of failure modes may be.

The more regular usage of partial availability will be around regular maintenance and system upgrades. The most valuable is when failure occurs. By implementing conceptual "bulkheads" in the system, only a portion of the system will fail. This can be valuable in reducing the pressure upon operators during remediation. Working on an outage of a critical system is always stressful. In adhering to this principle, the outage can be limited to only the affected subsystem, and thus only the users that depend upon that. This isn't a panacea, but it can be invaluable in relieving pressure on those working on an outage.

A succinct description of partial availability is being able to operate in a degraded state rather than a binary "up or down" status.

Design Flexibility

Flexibility in software is a squishy subject as there's no well-defined description of what flexible software *is*. My definition of design flexibility is that any facet of the system's design should have multiple options for implementation. In practice, I've found this to mean a consideration of what future paths the software may take, and to the extent possible, not *excluding* those possibilities.

The future, especially in a software project, is notoriously hard to predict. In alignment with the Agile Manifesto, this is responding to change rather than following a fixed plan. Our approach is to respond to change, design flexibility is about keeping options open for the future.

As a system matures there may be times where it is sensible to make decisions that would exclude certain future evolutionary paths. This is a culling of the design's flexibility. At that point, a certain wisdom on the project will have accrued which can minimize the impact of these decisions. This isn't a decision to make lightly, as reversing this type of decision can be costly. However, it can be the appropriate course of action in some situations.

When starting new projects, and especially in their early years, there is value to keeping future possibilities open. That is the essence of this principle.

Modularity

"Module" is an overloaded term. It is used in many domains in addition to software such as shelving, sofas, or even buildings. In each of these the grain, or specificity, of a module varies. However, the relationship of a module to the whole stands; modules are coarse subdivisions and may be recomposed with inclusion or exclusion to make new variations.

In software, microservices are the new modules. They're discrete pieces of functionality, packaged up as independently deployable units. That last part isn't required though. The now-maligned "monolith" architecture, where there's a single deployable unit, doesn't mean that the internals of the system are composed like a bowl of spaghetti. Following the microservices trend without paying attention to the overall architecture leads to *distributed* spaghetti. How units of software are composed still matters.

The answer to this is creating a modular system, where modules interact in specified ways. Deployment of the modules is a separate concern; one extreme is one module per deployable unit, a microservices architecture. The other extreme is a monolith, or as some have coined, a "modulith[3]."

The principle of modularity is to avoid a spaghetti system. Independent of deployment units, a system must be well factored into modules that make sense to the code as well as the business. Modules can be used as a dimension for deployment as well as parallelization of developer work.

By thinking of a system as modules, and then having modules communicate via asynchronous message passing, moving a module into a new deployment unit won't change the interaction pattern with the remainder of the system. Modularity is aligned with a reactive system.

Testability

Software will have bugs. I continue to make mistakes in the code I've written, and you will as well. To compensate, we test our work. Testing software is a rote task and well suited to automation. Testability is writing software such that writing automated tests is straightforward, lowering the barrier to writing them.

This principle is otherwise somewhat amorphous. What exactly *is* testability? I've found test-driven development (TDD) to be a mechanism to help me in my work. When starting with a test, you're starting as a consumer of the code you'll be writing. This consumer-first perspective of the API helps establish the boundaries of what the test will cover. This has an important interplay with modularity (tests should ideally be isolated to a module where possible) and the internal structure of modules themselves.

This principle is also well aligned with a reactive system. Boundaries where message passing occurs are also good boundaries for what an individual test will cover. The general goal is to encourage the writing of tests for our system.

---

[3] https://twitter.com/gernotstarke/status/901496976612655106

Amenability to Change

I saved my favorite principle for last. This phrasing, being amenable to change, is one that has been a repeating refrain in this book. A quip I once read can be paraphrased as:

May your system be in service long enough to be considered legacy.

"Legacy" tends to be a pejorative term when applied to software systems. It is not uncommon for working on legacy systems to be undesirable. Why is this? I believe it is related to this principle. Working on a system that isn't amenable to change is frustrating. It'll have a variety of factors that contribute to this, such as a lack of tests, intertwined business rules, and poor or no separation into modules. The system won't follow the prior principles laid out in this chapter.

The creation of a business application is an investment by the business. If an application that's less than a decade or two old needs to be rewritten, I believe that's often a failure in the system's architecture. That doesn't need to be the case.

In addition to setting the system up for long-term success, this is also in the spirit of agile development. By emphasizing working with the system's users to meet their needs, and acknowledging that changes will happen, amenability is an implicit requirement.

This philosophy is an aspect of the prior principles, and a principle in its own right. We want our work to be valued and contribute to the overall productivity of the business. This principle is to ensure that for the expected lifetime of our system. The dark side of this principle is over-engineering. *Amenable* has been carefully chosen. It isn't that every change must be simple or even straightforward. It's that the possibility of change has been considered, and the steps to achieve the change aren't counter to the fundamental constraints of the program.

Summary

This chapter has set the stage for our system's design. I've declared a few self-imposed constraints, and then a set of guiding principles for the design itself:

- GraphQL API

- Real-time UI updates

- Never Forget

- Message Driven

- Read/Write Separation

- Partial Availability

- Design Flexibility

- Modularity

- Testability

- Amenability to Change

With these in mind, the remainder of this part of the book will incrementally work toward the design of our system. The next chapter moves closer to implementation by introducing the high-level data flow and establishing some of the core modules.

CHAPTER 8

High-Level Data Flow

Given our self-imposed constraint of using GraphQL, in this chapter, we'll consider the high-level data flow of a system that utilizes it to back the API contract with user interfaces and other collaborating systems. I'll start with an explanation of Event Sourcing (ES) and Command Query Responsibility Segregation (CQRS), followed by a primer on how to think in terms of GraphQL's schema language, and finally bring all three concepts together.

Event Sourcing and CQRS

As alluded to when discussing time, we will be building a system that blends Event Sourcing (ES) and Command Query Responsibility Segregation (CQRS).

Event Sourcing was initially coined[1] by Martin Fowler in 2005. He is credited with giving it the name, but the idea certainly predated his writing on it. It is fundamentally a simple proposition: capture every change to an application's state as an event and use the collection of events as the source-of-truth for the application. Events have a natural order based on the sequence in which they occurred. This sequenced collection of events is termed an event log. The event log is the source-of-truth for the application, describing the sequence of changes that has occurred. While this is a natural way to record changes, it is not a natural mechanism for interrogating a system for its current state. To have a notion of the "current state," the event log is replayed to derive a state value.

The first event in an event log will be special, as it stands alone in time, depending on nothing. Every subsequent event builds upon the prior event. To derive a notion of "state," one must traverse the event log building up the concept by repeatedly incorporating the change each event represents. If you are familiar with functional

---

[1]www.martinfowler.com/eaaDev/EventSourcing.html

© Peter Royal 2023
P. Royal, *Building Modern Business Applications*, https://doi.org/10.1007/978-1-4842-8992-1_8

programming concepts, this is a fold. In Java's Stream library, it is a reduce. A benefit of this is that the state at any point in type may be reconstructed by terminating the operation at the desired point in time.

While Event Sourcing is useful for capturing changes to state, the event-based representation isn't natural for querying. Enter CQRS.

CQRS was championed by Udi Dahan[2] and Greg Young[3] at the end of the past decade, during the late 2000s. It is a very straightforward pattern: utilize separate models for commands (writes) and queries (reads). The CQRS pattern can be applied in any context, but it has been extremely popular when combined with Event Sourcing.

When combined, the event-sourced portion of the system handles writes. As events occur, the new event is incorporated (materialized) into a model for reads. Events are the natural communication method, as that's the output of Event Sourcing. This is further aligned with our desire to be a reactive system, being a message-driven interaction.

A missing detail from Event Sourcing is *what causes events to be created*. That is often left as "an exercise for the reader," so to speak. Fear not, this book has an answer. Prior to explaining the solution, I'm going to explain the decision to utilize GraphQL in more detail.

Thinking in GraphQL Schemas

The prior chapter had a brief introduction to GraphQL as part of explaining why it's a self-imposed constraint. A more detailed explanation is warranted to understand how it will interact with ES and CQRS.

A GraphQL schema represents a contract between the providing and consuming systems. The GraphQL community recommends starting with a "schema first" approach. A schema should be authored as the truest representation of the model possible with the language, rather than being a projection from an existing model into GraphQL. Understanding all the modeling capabilities in GraphQL is thus a necessary prerequisite.

---

[2] https://udidahan.com/2009/12/09/clarified-cqrs/

[3] http://codebetter.com/gregyoung/2010/02/16/cqrs-task-based-uis-event-sourcing-agh/

As the name implies, GraphQL is a graph structure. I'll describe the structure and available modeling primitives from the bottom up, starting with the leaves of the graph. All top-level names in a GraphQL schema occupy a shared namespace. In isolation, this isn't a problem. It is important to be aware of if consumers of your schema will be composing it with other schemas, as there is the potential for name collisions.

GraphQL requires callers to be explicit about what they request. There is no facility for "wildcarding" the data to return. When constructing a request, callers must specify the data they wish to see returned.

Scalars and Enums

At the lowest level, the leaves of the graph, there are two possibilities: scalar values and enums.

There's a small set of provided scalar types: strings, integers, floats, booleans, and object identifiers (IDs). It is also possible to define custom scalar types, as the provided primitives are insufficient for most models. Custom scalars are generally used for value types that are easily represented as single values, such as the various combinations of dates and times, URLs, and fixed-precision numbers. I also like to use custom scalars for value types specific to my model rather than relying on generic types such as String.

There are no provided enums (enumerations). GraphQL's enums are useful when modeling a value that must come from a fixed set. In contrast with the implementation of enums in some programming languages, GraphQL enums have no corresponding numerical value. Enum values aren't proxies for anything, they are values in their own right.

Objects

The simplest node type in the model is an object. Objects are named and are composed of one or more fields. Object names come from the shared namespace, but field names are local to the object definition. Fields return scalars, enums, or objects. There are a few additional possibilities that the subsequent subsections discuss.

A rough mental model is that an object is a bag of key and value pairs. That's accurate, but also insufficient. Fields of an object can declare optional and required arguments, giving them behavior of functions. A more apt mental model is to view an object as a bag of named functions.

Object fields can also specify a nullability constraint. The default is to allow any value to be nullable. While it may be tempting to use this to mirror existing constraints in your model, I recommend using it judiciously.

The execution model of GraphQL uses nullability as part of its error handling; if an error occurs during execution, the response will be converted to null starting at the point of the error toward the root of the query, stopping at the first nullable field. Extensive use of non-null increases the "blast radius" of errors. Using non-null also limits future evolution of the schema, as converting a field from non-null to nullable is considered a breaking change to the schema.

Lists

Lists are an augmentation to object fields. Any of the return values for an object's fields may be wrapped using a list construct, indicating that it will return potentially more than one value. A field's cardinality is either zero or one, and using a list expands that from zero to infinity. A list's values are homogenous.

The nullability constraint interacts with lists in two ways. Entries in the list can be declared as non-null, and the list itself may be declared as non-null. The error handling of the execution model is especially pertinent here. I recommend declaring the list value as nullable, as this allows other list values to be returned if an error occurs during execution.

Input Objects

Input objects are the mechanism for providing structure to object field arguments. Arguments must be one of the "primitive" values, a scalar or enum, or they may be organized into input objects.

An input object is a bag of key and value pairs. Input objects have fields, and the field values may be a scalar, enum, or another input object type. Values may be declared as a list, as well as being non-null.

In this context, nullability is more useful, as it communicates to users of the schema what the required arguments are. I recommend appropriately marking items as non-null, as it is the act of going from nullable to non-null that is a breaking change for callers.

Interfaces and Unions

Interfaces and unions are two organizational facets that I alluded to when introducing the object type. They each may be used when defining what the value type is for an object field.

Interfaces are a named set of fields that are shared across multiple object types. They are semantically equivalent to how interfaces behave in many programming languages. GraphQL's execution model allows callers to use interface fields directly, as well as having conditional behavior depending upon the concrete type. At execution time, interfaces must be satisfied by a concrete type. It is only the schema that defers that specific until execution. Interfaces may be implemented only by object types and other interfaces.

Unions are the opposite of interfaces. A union is a set of disjoint object types. Unions may not contain interfaces. They are semantically equivalent to a "Choice" or an "Either" type in programming languages. As the schema views them as a disjoint set, at execution time callers must indicate how each of the possibilities is to be handled.

Interfaces and unions are **not** available for use with input objects.

Queries and Subscriptions

Queries and subscriptions are two mechanisms for defining how to read data. They are each represented by a special type in the schema, the Query and Subscription types respectively. Generally, those names are used directly, but it is also possible to have custom names for them in your schema and map them to the two concepts.

Their definition is as an object type, and the same rules for object types apply here as well. The fields on these types make up the entry points to the model. It is common to see arguments used here, as it is a straightforward mechanism to access specific instances of a type.

The execution model of queries and subscriptions differ. For queries, callers can specify multiple fields to return. The GraphQL specification declares that an implementation may "resolve" (i.e., execute) these fields in parallel. For subscriptions, there are different semantics. When requesting a subscription field, exactly one field must be chosen. The implementation of a subscription field has hidden semantics where it is returning a sequence of the field's value type. This is the mechanism to provide real-time updates from a GraphQL system. Since the sequence is defined by the field's value type, using unions here is powerful as it allows for variation in what is returned in each "tick" of a subscription.

Mutations

Mutations are the mechanism for writing data. I find the implementation of writing in GraphQL to be rather clever, as it exploits the notion that each field is a conceptual function. Like queries and subscriptions, mutations are represented by a special type in the schema, the `Mutation` type.

As the mutation type is an object type, it is also using the same rules. Each field of this type is an available mutation, and the field's arguments are the mechanism for the callers to provide the values.

By convention, fields of this type are expected to mutate the state of the system. You may note that I've mentioned nothing prohibiting this in the prior sub-sections, and that is true. Similar to how it is a bad practice to implement an HTTP `GET` call that modifies state, the same is true for the fields of other object types, including the query and subscription types.

The execution model does provide an affordance in this area. Like queries, multiple fields from the mutation type may be requested by callers, as a means of invoking multiple mutations within a single request. If the same parallel execution model used with queries were applied, it would limit the usefulness of this capability as mutations wouldn't have a deterministic execution order. To address this, the execution model for the mutation type only is to resolve each field *serially*. This simplifies mental reconstruction of how mutations behave.

When reading data using GraphQL, the caller is "in charge." The schema dictates the available data, and the caller must specify what they want to receive. For mutations, the receiver is "in charge." The schema now dictates what the caller must supply. For reads, there is some ambiguity as to exactly what may be returned. Whenever an interface or union is present, that represents a set of possibilities. As those constructs aren't available for mutation inputs, the *exact* structure is declared in the schema, rather than the potential structure.

A common question I have encountered from developers new to GraphQL is "How can I reuse my output types as inputs for my mutation?". The simple (and unsatisfactory answer for them) is *you don't*. There is an intentional bifurcation between input and output types in GraphQL. Replicating the REST pattern of having the same payload shape used between GET, PUT, and POST operations is not made easy. I believe this is the GraphQL authors steering implementers toward certain interaction patterns.

The GraphQL community recommends that mutations should be as *specific as possible*. This is in contrast to REST APIs where a GET/PUT/POST trio often operate in concert using the same payload shape. By having specific mutations, the scope and side effects of a mutation are communicated clearly. When mutations involve workflows, this can be intention-revealing.

A pattern I've observed with REST APIs is the triggering of side effects based upon field changes. Consider an API for a system that is responsible for the payment of invoices. As new invoices are received, they are entered into the system. There is a workflow where users must approve and invoice, and after approval payment is automatically scheduled. The REST API implementation has a GET endpoint to retrieve an invoice and a POST to modify an invoice. There are multiple mutable fields on an invoice and for this example we're focusing on the status field. To approve an invoice, the status field is modified from "received" to "approved." Upon receiving this payload, the endpoint observes the change, and triggers the payment workflow. The workflow is a side effect of the POST. On its surface, the API definition doesn't indicate this will happen. Yes, it can be captured in documentation, but that won't be immediately visible in the calling codebase. It is possible to have a separate endpoint that makes this explicit. However, in practice, my observation is that this isn't always done.

Implementing the same interaction pattern in GraphQL isn't the most straightforward path, as there would need to be an object type that describes an Invoice and then a parallel InvoiceInput input type for a mutation. This can be incrementally better than a REST API, as the input type would only list the mutable fields. In addition to being *specific*, mutations should also be *sematic*. Following that advice, this example would have a mutation named approveAndPayInvoice, explicitly describing what it does. It intentionally obscures the relationship with the status field. Approving is an action unto itself. The act of approving updates the status field, rather than updating the status field triggering an action. This may be an inversion of how the API is conceptualized. I find it powerful.

I find the bifurcation of input and output types to be a valuable tool in API design. They are two sides to state: a request to change state and an observation of the state. This is similar to the state relationship between commands and events that was introduced in Chapter 6. The symmetry between input types and commands vs. output types and events is how we will combine GraphQL with Event Sourcing and CQRS

Combining GraphQL + ES + CQRS

As I mentioned in the earlier section on Event Sourcing, the ES pattern doesn't prescribe what causes events. I introduced the notion of a *command* in Chapter 6 when discussing time, and that is the concept that will be utilized here. I will explain how the pieces fit together, and then describe them in more detail.

GraphQL mutations should be *specific* and *semantic*. Mutations cleanly map to commands. Commands can be applied to the current state of the system yielding events to move the state forward in time. These events can be materialized into a view that corresponds to the GraphQL schema for queries. The events can also be used to drive GraphQL subscriptions, as we know precisely what has changed.

Event Sourcing drives the mutations. CQRS is the separation between the mutations and their model, described by input objects in the GraphQL schema, and queries and subscriptions which use the object types. This separation is well supported by the input and output type bifurcation in GraphQL and encourages us to model each side appropriately.

Starting from a mutation, there is a "command generator" that is responsible for deriving commands from mutations. There may not be a one-to-one mapping from a mutation to a command. Each mutation will generate one command, but multiple mutations may generate the same command, or a mutation may generate different commands depending upon its specific arguments. In the GraphQL schema, a mutation is effectively a function. The invocation of the function is encapsulated in a message, the command. Chapter 10 explores this component in detail.

Commands are a request for a change. There is a "command processor" that receives these requests and outputs events. The command processor is responsible for a category of business rules, those for "data at rest." The next chapter is focused on this component.

Events are received by an "event materializer" that is responsible for creating the model that will be used to satisfy GraphQL queries and subscriptions. Chapter 11 is an exploration of this component.

This yields a straightforward loop. Clients use queries to observe the state of the system. They then issue mutations to make changes. The command generator converts mutations into commands. These messages are then received by the command processor and generate events. Events are received by the event materializer and used to update the view that was used to satisfy client queries. The exterior of the system is a GraphQL interface. The interior is comprised of message passing, as either commands or events.

This data flow allows us to implement the interior as a reactive system, as it is fundamentally comprised of message passing.

Summary

In this chapter, we've learned about how GraphQL's schema language is an elegant fit for exposing a system built upon Event Sourcing and CQRS concepts. We've learned how to think in terms of a GraphQL schema, how Event Sourcing and CQRS are complementary, and how to combine all three of these concepts. We have a casual understanding of how data would flow through such a system.

In the next chapter, I'll explain the command processor component of this flow in greater detail.

CHAPTER 9

Command Processor

The command processor is a critical component of our system. It will be responsible for ensuring that a portion of our business rules, those for data at rest, will be enforced. In this chapter I explain the ideas behind this component, what will be required to construct it, how it works, how it fails, and how to test it. Let's dive in.

What It Is, and Is Not

The command processor is the event-sourced portion of the system. It is responsible for orchestrating the creation of the events that comprise the system's state. As a part of this it also enforces a category of business rules, the rules for data at rest. Events describe the past, things that have occurred. In order to validly create events, it is necessary to ensure that they satisfy the business rules that were in effect at that time.

In the system this book describes, there is a single command processor that processes events in serial. This is a trade-off, and one that other implementations of event sourcing may not choose to take. I believe a single command processor simplifies a system, especially in the earlier stages. This is a deferrable decision. If a single command processor is unable to keep pace with incoming commands, there is a path toward parallelization. However, care must be taken when going down that path as some constraints upon the system will be more difficult to enforce. For the scale that many business applications operate at, I believe the simpler solution is preferable. I prefer to defer complexity until it is warranted but at the same time thinking ahead to consider how it may be handled as to not preclude the possibility in a design.

© Peter Royal 2023
P. Royal, *Building Modern Business Applications*, https://doi.org/10.1007/978-1-4842-8992-1_9

Requirements

Commands and events are each a type of message. In the prior chapter, I explained that the sequenced set of events is termed an event log. It then follows that a generalization of this for any type of message can be termed a message log.

The command processor receives commands as inputs, and outputs zero or more events for each command. To simplify the operation of this component, commands will be received from a message log, the command log. More details on writing to the command log are in the next chapter, as a part of the command generator. For the purposes of the command processor and this chapter, the command log is the ordered set of commands that are awaiting processing.

This act of storing commands into a command log is another existing practice that is, unsurprisingly, named command sourcing. In this book's system, I am combining these two practices. Commands are sourced in order to generate events, and events are sourced in order to generate the official state of the system. Going from a command to events is akin to a mapping function from the command log to the event log. The next section on composing the core loop expands upon this idea.

After processing a command, the system doesn't have a specific need to retain the command. While the event log must be persisted across all time, processed commands can be discarded. However, there are benefits to retaining them that the section on testing later in this chapter will explore.

The command processor is enforcing one of the categorizations of business rules I described in Chapter 5, those for data at rest. This is a critical responsibility of the command processor. For the proposed means of operation of this component, it is critical that the generation of events is *free from side effects*. Side effects are a separate category of business rules and must come after generating events, not as a part of the process that generates them. Side effects take two forms. The common one that often comes to mind is the case of a notification. Something happened, and we need to let another system know. This form is akin to a function that returns void; it's "fire and forget." The sometimes-overlooked category of side effects is the side effects that consult another source of state and return something from that state. It is critical to realize that these interactions are *also* side effects. A command represents a request to change the state of the system. In order to be an accurate representation, a command must be a complete representation of *all* information needed to fulfill the request. If there is data validation that involves a state that is external to the command processor, that state must be consulted as a part of command generation, not command processing.

This makes a short list of requirements for the command processor that I will use in the next section as part of composing its processing loop:

- Commands are sourced from a command log.

- Processing commands is a mapping function from the command log to the event log.

- The mapping function must be free from side effects.

Composing the Core Loop

It is useful to view the command processor as a loop. Given a command and the current state of the system, call a function that takes those two data points as inputs and returns a list of new events as output. As new commands arrive, repeat. The command log supplies the system with new commands, but where does the current state come from? In an event-sourced system such as this one, there is no single "current state." Changes to the state are spread across the event log. In order to process commands, it is necessary to derive this view of the "current state."

Since the command processor is only responsible for enforcing the business rules for data at rest, its view of the current state is a subset of all the information contained within the events. Its current state only needs to contain the information necessary to enforce the rules.

Message logs are infinite streams. For the event log, every event implies a new version of the "current state." To achieve this, I will use a concept from stream processing, a scan operator. This is a type of folding function. Folding functions are a type of higher-order function used to recursively analyze data structures. You may be familiar with this concept via the name that it is commonly available as in many standard libraries, reduce. A folding function requires two inputs: an initial value, and a function that accepts two arguments, an element from the data structure and the initial value, yielding the next value. This function is repeatedly invoked for every element in the data structure, with the return value from one invocation being the initial value for the next. After all elements of the data structure had been exhausted, the final return value is used as the folding functions return value.

Computing the sum of a list of integers is an example of a folding function. Given a list of numbers:

```
[1,3,5,7,9]
```

To compute the sum, we would invoke a reduce function as follows:

```
reduce([1,3,5,7,9], 0, (state, item) => state + item)
```

The return value of reduce would be 25. The third argument is our "reducing" function. The first argument is the state of the reduction, and when processing the first item of the list, it will be the initial value, 0. The second argument is the current item from the list. Unrolling the internal loop that reduce is performing would be akin to:

```
reducer = (state, item) => state + item
result = 0
result = reducer(result, 1) # result is 1
result = reducer(result, 3) # result is 4
result = reducer(result, 5) # result is 9
result = reducer(result, 7) # result is 16
result = reducer(result, 9) # result is 25
```

Seeing the unrolled form may allow your eyes to realize the trick that scan performs. Since scan is operating upon a stream, it can generate an output stream based on the incremental values of result. The output stream starts with the initial value, and then for each element in the input stream the output contains the result of applying the reducing function to the prior element of the output stream plus the next element of the input stream.

When applied to an event log, scan can be used to derive a state value after every event. The initial value is the state of the system before any events are added. The reducer is then invoked with the prior state and the next event. With this, the event log is mapped to a stream of system states.

The core loop is now able to be expressed in terms of stream processing. We have two streams: the command log and the event log. The event log can be mapped into a stream representing system states using a scan operation. These two streams, the stream of states and the stream of commands, can then be "zipped" together to create a stream of events, our event log! "Zipping" is another stream processing operation that borrows its name from the device you'll find in clothing, the zipper. A physical zipper takes its two sides of teeth and "zips" them together, taking one from each side and joining them.

A `zip` operation in stream processing is the pairwise combination of two streams, calling a function with the element of each stream, and then creating a new stream comprised of those return values.

The core loop requires two stream processing primitives, `zip` and `scan`, and two functions specific to our domain. The function that builds state from events will be termed the *applicator*, as it is applying an event to the current state. The function that uses state plus a command to generate events will be termed the *mutator*, as it is mutating state via the command.

Given our requirement that these functions are free from side effects, they are pure functions. A pure function is a function that will always return the same outputs given the same inputs. Pure functions are very amenable to testing, which is the focus of a section later in this chapter.

With the core loop represented as operations upon a stream of messages, it is aligned with our principle, and the reactive system property, of being message driven. Although the core is straightforward, there are some additional complexities that will be layered in as a part of handling failure scenarios.

Handling Failures

There are two facets to the command processor. The first facet is comprised of the two domain-specific functions: the mutator and the applicator. The second facet is everything else, the conceptual plumbing of the streams through our metaphorical pipes.

Each facet is a discrete concern. The first facet is an application concern, and the second facet is infrastructure. In separating these concerns, each can have the appropriate failure handling policies.

Infrastructure

Failure handling in the infrastructure facet is a simple strategy. If the failure is something that is retriable, retry the operation. If it is not retriable, or the retries are bounded, then "fail upstream," allowing whatever is orchestrating the command processor's execution to handle the failure.

The types of failures that may occur will likely be centered around I/O – when reading commands and events as part of the processor's inputs, or when writing new events to the event log. If the function used to generate events is allowed to generate multiple events per command, it is necessary to ensure that writing to the event log is transactional. Either all the generated events are written, or none are. If the event log is not transactional and multiple events are written, a failure in the middle would leave the system in an inconsistent state; the command is effectively partially processed, which is invalid.

A failure when executing one of the two domain-specific functions is *not* an infrastructure failure. As the functions are pure, they are retriable as needed by retries due to an infrastructure failure. Otherwise, they require discrete handling as the nature of their failures are categorically different.

Application

A failure in one of the two domain-specific functions won't be solved with a naive retry. As the functions are stateless, a failure indicates a problem with either the inputs or a logic error in the function itself. There are two broad categorizations of failures from these functions, a failure related to processing a new command, or a failure in constructing state from existing events.

The simpler case is a failure in constructing state from existing events. Categorically, this should not occur. As the existing events are the truth of the system, they need to be viewed as such. Yes, it is possible that they contain "bad" information of some sort due to prior logic bugs, but that should be considered an exceptional situation. The function that derives state needs to appropriately handle these events. Chapter 12 will discuss testing techniques to help minimize the chances of this occurring.

The remaining cases of application failure then center around the processing of commands. Failure here is different, failure is *expected* and *normal*. Whenever a command would put the system in a state where one of the rules for data at rest would be violated, it would need to be rejected. Remember, a command is ultimately a request to change the state of the system. It is not pre-ordained that the request will succeed. (It is here that the usage of the term command starts to be stretched. While commands are authoritative orders, it is ok for the system to say "no").

Commands will originate from someone that wants to change the state of the system, most likely a user. As commands are requests, the originators will want to know the disposition of their request. To achieve this, it is necessary to additionally record this disposition into another message log, a processed command log. The processed command log contains an entry for every command indicating whether it succeeded or failed. After submitting a command, this log can be watched to determine whether the command was a success.

The processed command log also plays a role in the core loop. There are three pieces of data an entry in this log contains:

1. Pointer into the command log to the command that was processed

2. Disposition of the command, whether it succeeded or failed

3. Pointer into the event log indicating the most recent event after processing

These data points are correlated but used for differing purposes. The pointer into the command log is the state keeping as to which commands have been processed. The disposition of the command allows for the command's originators to observe the result. The event log pointer allows for commands to generate multiple events.

I haven't explicitly mentioned commands generating multiple events. It is a useful practice, as it allows events to be finer grained than commands and for multiple commands to generate the same event. The benefit is for the consumers of the event log. With fine-grained events, the logic that backs each event can be more discrete with minimal overlap between events. A command generating multiple events represents a wrinkle with the core loop. When I originally introduced the core loop, I described how the event log would be used to generate a state after each event and those states would be "zipped" with the commands. If there's a one-to-one correspondence between commands and events, that zipping process is straightforward; after processing a command, there will be one new state generated which is ready to be used for the next command. When commands generate multiple events, there will be multiple states generated. How will the loop know which one is the correct one to use for the next command? That's the purpose of the pointer into the event log. The derived stream of states is joined with the processed command log to sample the state stream, so it *only* contains states that occur after all events a command generated have been applied. This allows for reuse of the state when a command fails; a processed command for a failed command will contain the *same event log pointer* as the prior processed command because there *are no new events*.

Enforcing Business Rules

The enforcement of business rules for data at rest presents an opportunity for failure. When the command processor state is constructed, events are repeatedly applied onto the state. Each time this occurs is an opportunity to ensure that the next event will not generate an invalid state. Between the two functions that are supplied to the command processor, the applicator is the appropriate place to ensure that all generated states are valid. For events in the event log, this function should always succeed. If it fails, it is an indication of an error in the system. Perhaps the events have been tampered with, or perhaps the business rules have changed, and older events no longer satisfy the new rules.

If the business rules haven't changed, a failure to generate a state from existing events will require operator intervention. If the business rules *have* changed, the change needs to be appropriately captured. I had discussed this previously in Chapter 6. A business rule change occurs at a point in time. It is necessary to record that change *as an event*. The function that is generating state from events is then able to use this business rule change event to alter its behavior.

When processing a new command, it is necessary to ensure that the events it generates satisfy the business rules. In order to avoid duplication of business rule enforcement, after calling the mutator function, the command processor will also use the applicator to ensure that when the prospective events are applied to the current state that they are able to create a new state without failing.

In practice, I find that most command failures will end up occurring when ensuring that they are able to generate valid states. If the command is a request to make a change, the events generated from the command are the planned steps necessary in order to realize the change. It is only after those events have been successfully applied to the state can the plan be considered a success.

This application of events to state as part of processing a command is *prospective*. The new state generated is discarded, as the state used for the next command will come from following the event log. This is possible because the function is free from side effects.

Intimately related to handling failures is the minimization of unexpected scenarios. That's best done by thorough testing.

How to Test

I've found that the separation of concerns in the command processor is extremely amenable to testing. The processor takes in two functions in order to operate with specific command and event types. This allows testing to be split into the testing of the command processor itself, and then the testing of the domain-specific functions.

Testing the Command Processor

The mechanics of the command processor itself should be tested with a simplistic domain, such as adding numbers. Commands are representable as integers, a number that the current state should equal. The mutator can then generate an event that is another integer, the integer that must be added to the current state in order to have it equal the command value. The applicator is an addition. A simplistic business rule may be added, such as the state value must always be an odd number.

By using a simple domain, it's then possible to stress test the command processor to see how it behaves in various failure scenarios. As its means of operation are expressible in terms of stream processing, if the implementation makes use of a library that has the necessary primitives, testing is primarily an exercise in ensuring that the library has been used correctly and that other collaborating components compose as expected.

Testing Your Code

There are two functions to test, the applicator and the mutator. Each may be tested individually in isolation, without requiring the command processor. This is a benefit of the requirement that they are pure functions. All necessary information for them to perform is provided as arguments.

For the applicator, there should be at least one test per event to ensure that the state is updated as expected for valid events. In practice, there will likely be a handful of tests for each event to cover the business rules that the change impacts. Notably, the implementation of the application should be mostly free of conditional logic, other than the business rule constraint checks. The applicator is applying events to state. The events are looking backward, describing what has already happened. Conditionals should only be used to ensure that what happened was valid. If you find yourself writing conditional behavior that's not related to checking the business rule constraints, that's a hint that the logic belongs in the mutator function.

The mutator is the function that will contain branching decision logic. The mutator inputs are a command and the current state, and it returns a set of events to describe how to move the state forward in time. It is entirely appropriate for the command to use information contained with the state to guide its behavior and alter the set of events returned. Like the applicator, there should be at least one test per command. The actual number of tests will end up varying based on the branching logic within the mutator for a given command. It is feasible to exhaustively cover all the possible scenarios for a given command. The tests can also ensure that the command's returned events will pass the applicator when provided with the events and the same state that the mutator was provided with. It's possible and recommended to do this without using the command processor itself, as ultimately it is merely orchestrating the execution of the mutator and the applicator.

Testing these functions within the context of the command processor will be covered later in Chapter 12.

There's an additional type of test that can be performed, a regression test against production data. In a strict sense, commands in the command log don't need to be retained after they've been processed. However, retaining commands allows for using them in tests. Commands can be reprocessed with newer versions of the mutator to ensure that the same events are generated. This is a powerful technique for ensuring that drastic refactoring of system logic results in a system with the exact same behaviors.

Summary

The command processor sits at the heart of our system, enforcing some of the most important business rules, the rules for data at rest. I've explained the essence of its operating principles, and what is required for its operation. You've learned how to think about testing the component as well as testing your commands and events in conjunction with it. The next chapter will give the same treatment to the command generator, which is responsible for creation of the commands that the command processor operates upon.

CHAPTER 10

Command Generator

The command generator is the bridge between the outwardly facing request/
response interactions of GraphQL mutations and the message passing world inside
the application. In this chapter, I discuss how GraphQL mutations interact with the
command generator and the balance between specificity and generality when designing
commands and mutations. I will also go over how to construct commands that allow
the command processor's mutator function to be a pure function, how the command
generator can fail and how to compensate, and finally how to think about testing the
logic contained in this layer. Let's dive in.

Interaction with GraphQL

The command generator is the logical component that allows our GraphQL mutations to
function. Its behavior is decomposable into the following three steps:

1. Convert the GraphQL mutation's input arguments into a
   command.

2. Append the command to the command log.

3. Awaiting processing of the command and returning the
   disposition as the mutation's result.

From Input Arguments into a Command

A mutation represents a single transaction within our system. This follows from the
behavior of the command processor, where it processes commands one at a time.
The additional complexity of a "composite command" that could contain multiple
commands has been intentionally omitted. Some aspects to this complexity include
whether nesting of composite commands should be allowed, and a limit to the number

of commands within a composite command. While this complexity may be warranted in some situations, I believe making discrete commands that match the needs of the system's users is a simpler approach.

A single GraphQL request to our system may invoke multiple mutations because GraphQL allows callers to request multiple fields in query and mutation requests. If callers make use of this feature, each one will be serially handled in the order they were specified in the request. The GraphQL specification does not permit asynchronous execution of mutations as it would be difficult to reason about the order in which changes were made. In practice, I have not seen this feature extensively used for mutations as it is semantically equivalent to multiple requests. The GraphQL specification has no opinion on how multiple mutations in a single request should potentially all succeed or fail. If a request invokes a single mutation, it is easier to reason about failure scenarios and manage on the caller side.

In our system, a mutation will generate at most one command. As you map mutations to commands, you may find that a command is reused across multiple mutations. I find this to be a good thing, having generality in the implementation of the system while exposing a more specific interface. Arguments to the command may be implicit in the described behavior of the mutation.

When designing your GraphQL schema, you should specify as many non-null constraints for the input as feasible given the modeling limitations with GraphQL. A limitation you may encounter is the lack of unions on input types. If you have an input object where you want callers to specify at most a single field of the type, there's no language facility to indicate it in the schema. As of this writing, there is an open RFC to the GraphQL specification to add a @oneOf directive to input objects to support a limited form of polymorphism for input objects.

The first step in creating a command is performing additional validations upon the input values that were inexpressible in the schema. This may include criteria such as number range restrictions, string length checks, and anything else that is required for a command to be considered "valid." In your implementation, it is possible to create a custom directive to allow the specification of these constraints within your schema. This would allow your implementation to use these directives to drive validation as well as being descriptive in the schema.

Conceptually, all validation required for a command to be "fully formed" are a part of this step. The validation in this step is structural only and akin to completing all fields on a form without consideration as to whether the values are semantically correct. Just as the caller completed all fields in the mutation's arguments as part of its invocation, the command generator needs to create a complete command prior to appending it to the command log. After the command has been added to the log there will not be an opportunity for the system to adjust what the command implies.

The GraphQL community generally recommends having mutations be as specific as possible. The key part of that advice is *as possible*. At one extreme is a schema with a single mutation that is intended to handle any scenario. I hope that this sounds at a minimum confusing, and ideally nonsensical. Such a schema would require extensive documentation on how to invoke it for specific scenarios. The intent of the community guidance is to try and have the schema itself be self-documenting for the mutation. In having specific mutations, the mutation name itself is an indicator of the operation it will perform.

When creating GraphQL schema, I start with making all mutations as specific as possible and mirror that specificity in the generated commands. Then, as callers start to get a feel for how the schema fits into their workflows, there may be cases where the scope of some mutations will be increased.

As an example, consider the following two mutations (ignore their return values for now):

```
input CreateCustomerInput {
    name: String!
}

input UpdateCustomerRegionInput {
    customerId: ID!
    regionId: ID!
}

type Mutation {
    createCustomer(input: CreateCustomerInput!): Boolean
    updateCustomerRegion(input: UpdateCustomerRegionInput!): Boolean
}
```

In this hypothetical system, there are customers that exist in regions. Newly created customers have no associated region until one has been assigned. In practice, the user interface flow for creating a customer always calls updateCustomerRegion after creating a customer. Thus, it is reasonable to add an optional regionId to the

`CreateCustomerInput` type allowing for a simpler interaction pattern for callers. It is this pragmatic use-case-driven generalization of mutations that I support. The goal of any generalization should be to solve an actual pain point for users of the schema. This should be balanced with the goal of specificity, to avoid coupling between callers and the implementation. Specific mutations theoretically allow callers to compose their flows as they see fit.

Appending to the Command Log

After a command has been created, it needs to be appended to the command log for the command processing engine to act upon it. It is here that the order of commands is established. If the system receives two mutations contemporaneously, it is the order that they are appended to the command log that defines the order that they will be processed in.

The act of appending the command is also an opportunity to perform another validation, the rejection of duplicate requests. Imagine a scenario where a caller sends a request for a mutation but then experiences a network interruption and is unable to receive the response. How can the caller ensure that their request was handled? If the caller were to resend their request, there could be side effects that this request implies that would be undesirable to duplicate. We need a mechanism to allow for client requests to be *idempotent*. Strict, by-the-book idempotency is infeasible for mutations, as the intent of a mutation is to generate a side effect. It is a valid scenario to invoke a mutation multiple times with the intent of triggering the side effect multiple times. To handle these two scenarios, the intentional and unintentional repetition of a mutation, we will introduce a new argument to each mutation, a client request identifier.

The client request identifier, abbreviated as a `requestId`, is a value that is unique for every logical request. If a client intends to invoke a mutation five times, they will need to supply five distinct IDs. However, if a client invokes a mutation and experiences a network interruption and is unsure if it was accepted by the system, they should resend the request with the *same* ID.

An ideal location for checking whether a `requestId` has been previously observed is when attempting to append the command to the command log. By having the command log also track that set of observed IDs, duplicate requests can be detected.

If a duplicate request is observed, how should the system behave? I lean toward treating it as a failure for the duplicate request. The caller knows whether they have retried a request. If a retried request fails because the requestId has already been used, the caller has the context to understand what occurred. If this failure occurs for a request that the caller hasn't repeated, there is something else afoot that will need to be investigated. Perhaps there is a logic error in the system, or the generation of IDs across clients isn't sufficiently unique.

If an expected duplicate request is observed, how can the caller learn of the disposition of the original request? The requestId is a unique identifier that can be used to look up the prior disposition. My preferred mechanism is to have a query that can be called to return the disposition of any prior requestId. The alternative is to have the duplicate request return a variation upon the success case, a "this request has already been executed." The frequency at which this occurs will likely guide your choice. For business applications that are usually used by users that are in relatively fixed locations, duplicate requests due to network disruptions will be rarer compared to a business application used on a mobile device.

Returning the Mutation Result

The final step of the mutation flow is to return the result of the mutation to the caller. After successfully appending the command to the command log, it will become visible to the command processor. As described in the prior chapter, there is an additional message log, the processed command log, that directly relates a command to its result. This message log will be temporarily subscribed to in order to observe the mutation result.

There is a *critical* timing nuance here. Your code needs to subscribe to the processed command log *before* appending the command to the command log. If the order is reversed, you risk missing the event if the command processor completes before the processed command log subscription is active.

The processed command log contains results for all commands. We need a mechanism to filter the results for the command we have appended. The interaction with our caller is a request/response interaction, and that is the same pattern that is used with the command processing engine. However, with the command processing engine, it is indirect as we are appending to one message log and observing the result on another. My solution is to use the envelope pattern.

The envelope pattern is when you wrap your messages in an envelope, just as you would when sending a letter using the postal service. The command log doesn't contain commands, it contains commands wrapped in envelopes. When the command processor processes a command and appends to the processed command log, it *reuses* the envelope that the command arrived in. Since there is a one-to-one relationship between commands and processed commands, this is a straightforward operation. Reusing the envelope with the event log would be tricker, as a command can generate multiple events. We would then need policies for how to safely duplicate envelopes, complexity that I prefer to avoid if possible.

With the envelope pattern in place, the command generator can place a unique identifier (such as a UUID) on the envelope prior to appending to the command log. The processed command log results can then be filtered by this identifier to find the processed command that corresponds to our command. This is a distinct value from the requestId, as it is globally unique within the system. It identifies a specific command, even if the command is a logical duplicate due to the reuse of the requestId.

A processed command contains the sequence number corresponding to our command, the maximum sequence number for any generated events, and the result of the command, whether it succeeded or failed. This information will be used to construct the mutation result.

Failures will be communicated to callers via types in the GraphQL schema rather than using GraphQL's error mechanism. This is because errors in GraphQL are *untyped*. The GraphQL specification defines how errors appear in a response, but there are no facilities for describing their structure. I view this as a steering mechanism. Mutation failures will ultimately need to be communicated to users. As a business application, there will be mutations that fail because the change would violate the system's business rules. When this situation happens, it is critical to communicate as much detail about the violation to users, so they understand the nature of the violation and can correct the input.

I prefer to structure the return type of my mutations as a union between success and failure:

```
union MutationResult = MutationSuccess | MutationFailed
```

The MutationFailed type is a container to hold additional details. Just as how your data is modeled in the GraphQL schema, the ways in which your business rules can be violated should be modeled in the schema.

My preferred mechanism is to have an enumeration that indicates a class of errors, and then a field that implements an interface with more specific details. Recall the example from earlier in this chapter:

```
input CreateCustomerInput {
    name: String!
}

input UpdateCustomerRegionInput {
    customerId: ID!
    regionId: ID!
}

type Mutation {
    createCustomer(input: CreateCustomerInput!): Boolean
    updateCustomerRegion(input: UpdateCustomerRegionInput!): Boolean
}
```

Rather than returning a Boolean, it can be structured like the following:

```
enum MutationFailureCode {
  DUPLICATE_REQUEST_ID
  BUSINESS_RULE_VIOLATION
  UNKNOWN
}

interface MutationFailureDetails {
  message: String
}

type GenericMutationFailureDetails implements MutationFailureDetails {
  message: String
}

type InvalidCustomerName implements MutationFailureDetails {
  message: String
}

type MutationFailed {
  code: MutationFailureCode!
  details: MutationFailureDetails
}
```

```
union MutationResult = MutationSuccess | MutationFailed

input CreateCustomerInput {
    name: String!
}

type Mutation {
    createCustomer(input: CreateCustomerInput!): MutationResult
}
```

In this example, there are business rules around a new customer's name. In order to communicate to callers when these rules are violated, a specific InvalidCustomerName type is used. I also added a value to the MutationFailureCode enumeration, DUPLICATE_REQUEST_ID. This code can be used to signal duplicate requestId values, a topic discussed earlier in this chapter.

When a mutation results in successful command processing, there is only one piece of information to return: the sequence number of the final event. This yields a straightforward MutationSuccess type:

```
type MutationSuccess {
  visibleAsOfRevision: Int!
}
```

This pattern differs from other recommendations on how to design GraphQL mutations. This is intentional as our system here is an event-driven one. The successful processing of the command does *not* mean that the view has been updated; that's the responsibility of the Event Materializer, the topic of the next chapter.

This *does* mean that the eventually consistent nature of the system is exposed externally. I believe there is power in that. One of the design principles is to enable real-time UI updates. When using GraphQL, this is accomplished by using GraphQL's subscription mechanism. If a caller has an active subscription and then submits a mutation, there is no need to reflect any data changes in direct response to the mutation. When the view has been updated, the established subscription will relay the changes. By including event sequence numbers in the view model, callers can compare those values to the visibleAsOfRevision mutation result to know when the mutation's changes have been incorporated into the view.

Commands and Other Required Data

The input for a mutation may not always contain all the information necessary to construct a command. As the command processor's mutator function needs to be a pure function, any additional processing needs to occur prior to creating the command and submitting it for processing.

The work performed prior to submitting a command should be safe to retry. If there is an interruption in the network, clients may resubmit a mutation leading to re-execution of any work performed in the creation of a command.

This stage should be thought of as enriching the data received in order to satisfy the first category of business rules, those for data at rest. Any business rule side effects should occur after the command has been successfully processed.

As an example, consider a mutation that accepts tabular data. One approach is to have the data broken out into rows and columns by using arrays of input objects. However, what if the data was authored by users in a spreadsheet? It may make more sense to have the users upload the spreadsheet to the system and have it extract the tabular data. That extraction would occur as a part of command generation.

Another example is a file upload where the contents of the file are irrelevant to the system. The command generator can receive the file and store its contents into an object store, such as Amazon's S3. The command then contains only a reference to the object store.

Handling Failures

There are multiple ways for command generation and submission to fail. I have already touched on two of them in this chapter, input validation for constraints that are inexpressible in a GraphQL schema, and the client-supplied idempotency token, the requestId.

The failure opportunities for the creation of a command from input arguments will depend upon the nature and complexity of the process. Aside from handling invalid input, failures are likely to occur from software bugs in the implementation, something that tests can help alleviate.

Appending the new command to the command log could fail if the command log is unable to accept writes. This failure should be communicated as the system being unavailable so that clients can retry their requests.

There are also two cases where we may want to induce failures, an implementation of optimistic locking and timeouts.

Optimistic Locking

When making changes to data, users are aware of the current state. This breaks down in a multiuser system. What if two users are making changes to the same piece of data contemporaneously? In our system here, the user whose command is appended to the command log second will "win." The first change isn't "lost" because the events are persisted in the event log. When this happens it will be unexpected for the user that made the first change as they may have taken a different action with knowledge of the second change (and vice versa). Fortunately, there is a straightforward solution to this problem within our system, optimistic locking.

The premise of optimistic locking is to avoid the need for exclusive locks by tracking whether there are simultaneous modifications to data. In our request/response-based system, we need a value that callers can supply for their mutations that allow the system to determine whether the data has been changed. We can easily generate such a value for our system using the event log. It is already sequential, an essential property for its correctness. Every event will be assigned an increasing number, the sequence number. The functions you supply to the command processor can then make use of this value. When the applicator function applies an event to the state to produce a new state, it can also store the sequence number of the event in the state. Your event materializer, described in the next chapter, can make this sequence number visible in your GraphQL schema. This will allow callers to know the last modified revision, internally the sequence number, for a piece of data in the schema. This revision number can then be passed as another input argument to mutations as a means of indicating what revision a user was looking at when making a change. From a mutation perspective, the change is being made "as of" a specific revision. It can be stored in the command's envelope as an "as of revision." Finally, the mutator function within the command processor can make use of this value to see if the relevant state has a larger sequence value than the provided as of revision.

This check can be as coarse or fine-grained as your system requires. You can also mandate its usage by clients or allow its checking to be optional. If this check fails, it is an induced failure. It is important to distinguish these failures from others to callers, as user intervention will be required to determine what the next course of action will be. A user may decide to resubmit their mutation with an updated as-of-revision or they may abandon the change entirely.

Timeouts

In an eventually consistent system such as this one, it is important to prevent eventually from being too far into the future. Users of the system value a deterministic response time, even if the response is a failure. While we can't prevent all failures that could occur, we can provide bounded wait times by using timeouts. This ensures responsiveness, a principle I discussed in Chapter 3.

There are two places in the command generator to enforce timeouts: the submission of a command and awaiting the command's disposition from the command processor. It is beneficial to distinguish these two failures to callers, as the compensating action they will perform is different for each.

If there is a timeout awaiting the command processor, we know that the command was successfully submitted. How to handle this failure will depend upon the frequency at which you observe it and the criticality of surfacing it to your users. The simple solution here is to do nothing to compensate. Yes, a timeout occurred, but the system was able to eventually recover and process the change. If the caller was ultimately a human user of the system, they may have moved on with their work and the observation of the change will be sufficient for them to determine whether to manually retry. If the mutation is being made by another system, or if it is part of a workflow that requires users to explicitly observe success, then a more sophisticated approach is warranted. The requestId value will be used to add a new GraphQL query that returns the MutationResult for the request. I mentioned earlier in this chapter that the envelope that a command is placed in can be reused for the eventual processed command. This means that the requestId will also be available on the processed command. The happy path described previously was to use a per-command unique value on the command's envelope to filter processed commands. Since the processed command envelope will also contain the requestId, processed commands can also be filtered by this value. This new query can then be polled by clients to observe the command's disposition. This new query should also have a timeout, so callers will need to be prepared to retry as necessary. Another approach is to use a GraphQL subscription. The subscription signature will be the same as the query. The benefit of using a subscription is that the transport for subscriptions will likely have a keep-alive mechanism while the connection is quiescent, allowing callers to distinguish awaiting a response vs. the system being nonresponsive.

For timeouts submitting a command, callers will not know whether the submission was successful or not. The solution for this was discussed earlier in this chapter, the `requestId`. Callers can invoke the mutation again providing the same `requestId` value. The result of this subsequent attempt will provide information about the first attempt. If the attempt succeeds, the prior command wasn't successfully submitted. If the attempt fails due to duplicate `requestId`, then the caller knows that the prior command was successfully submitted.

A command submission timeout followed by a failure due to an already used `requestId` means that the command *was* successfully submitted. In this scenario, callers can use the same mechanism I described for processing timeouts to determine the command's disposition.

Testing the Command Generator

The command generator can be thought of in two parts. First, the generic infrastructure for command submission and awaiting the result of the command processor, and second, your domain logic for converting mutation inputs into a command, the creation of a command.

Command Submission

The act of submitting a command and waiting for the processing result is a mechanical action divorced from your domain logic. I like processes such as these as they provide a separation of concerns between application infrastructure and business rules. The rules for this process are strict and limited. There is only one piece of input data that has a rule, the `requestId`.

When writing tests for this process I like to use commands from an imaginary domain unrelated to the business problem at hand. This ensures that changes to domain types won't have any changes to this portion of my codebase, and as a bonus provides an opportunity for a bit of fun. I'll often personalize my tests a bit by using examples related to my pets. For command submission, the commands used in test could relate to adopting new pets, usually using the names and types of pets I've had over the years.

When testing command submission, I will write a happy-path test for submitting a command and the filtering of processed commands. I will not use a real command processing engine for these tests, instead using stub instances that I can control in test. I value the creation of interfaces that represent the API contracts between these components of the system. The act of using sub implementations of the API interfaces reinforces a separation of concerns between these components of the system as well as strict control of the coupling between them.

It is also important to test the failure modes of this process. The stub implementations you create should support failure injection so you can ensure that the system will behave as expected when failures occur. The happy-path testing will be well exercised by the testing I describe in Chapter 12. Those tests are unlikely to expose the failure modes that may be observed in production and ensuring that callers have a good experience in the face of failure is important toward providing a responsive and resilient system.

Command Creation

Each GraphQL mutation *could* have a test created to ensure that it creates the expected command. In all honesty, I tend to not write these tests, allowing this sort of happy-path validation to occur as a part of the comprehensive system tests I will describe in Chapter 12. In most cases, the logic that is performed here will be a straightforward transformation from your mutation's input arguments into your command.

What is valuable to test here are the handling of invalid inputs, and any commands whose generation involves accessing external systems that could cause their own failures.

Every specific error type that is defined in your GraphQL schema should have a test that ensures that it is generated when expected. These tests should simulate the experience of the system's callers. This means that the tests may not be invoking the command creation process directly. Rather, they are indirectly invoking this process by calling into the GraphQL endpoint with an input that will exercise command creation and asserting the expected GraphQL response. I find this to be a pragmatic balance between ensuring the code behaves as expected, validating that the caller experience is as expected, and not over-authoring tests. If the underlying function to turn the inputs into a command is tested, there will still be a need to ensure that command creation failures are properly communicated to callers. I prefer to write tests to gain the necessary confidence in the system, and testing command creation from the GraphQL layer gives me that confidence.

An exception to this is command creation that relies on external systems where I need to inject failures in the tests. If the creation of a command requires communicating with another system, that is an opportunity for failure to occur. In order to keep our system responsive, we need to bound the execution time for external communication. This implies timeouts on any calls made, and determining whether retries should be performed, or perhaps relaying the failure to our callers and allowing them to determine when to retry. The specifics of these policies will depend upon the requirements of your system. There are no hard and fast rules on exactly what to do beyond the general rule of doing something to ensure responsiveness of our system.

Summary

You now understand how the command generator is the bridge between GraphQL mutations and the command processor. It is responsible for gathering the necessary information to create a wholly formed command, a critical step which allows the command processor's mutator function to be stateless and pure. You also understand how to begin to navigate the appropriate granularity for commands and what level of specific testing of this component is appropriate. As the command generator only returns a sequence number upon successful mutations, the next chapter on the event materializer will be the bridge between the command processor's events and the views used to back GraphQL queries and subscription to allow callers to see the effect of their changes.

CHAPTER 11

Event Materializer

The event materializer is responsible for maintaining a stateful view model that will be used to satisfy GraphQL queries and subscriptions. In this chapter, I discuss how this component consumes from our system's event log and can also consume event streams from collaborating systems. I will also describe how this method of view maintenance allows for a straightforward implementation of GraphQL subscriptions. I will discuss how the event materializer can fail and how to test it to minimize those occurrences.

Defining the View Model

The view model that the event materializer maintains exists for the purpose of satisfying GraphQL requests. We can use this specificity to tailor the model for the queries that we have defined within our GraphQL schema. More concretely, the shape of the state stored within the view model should be very straightforward to pass to your GraphQL engine with minimal transformation. If you have denormalized data in your schema for ease-of-use by callers, also denormalize it in the storage model as well.

In Chapter 5 I discussed business rules, with one of the varieties being derivable data. Where possible, prefer to precompute this derived data instead of computing it on demand for every request. There are efficiency gains by doing work a single time. The system will be able to support a greater number of queries as each is less computationally expensive. It is possible to retain intermediate outputs for incremental computation, as well as storing different versions of the results as inputs change. The latter is valuable for debugging. If the time of a request is known, it will be possible to determine the data returned without recalculation.

Events should contain provenance information, when they were generated, the identity of who submitted the command they came from, and potentially other metadata that is useful in your domain. When materializing the view model, this information can be placed in the appropriate locations to communicate to users who last touched

© Peter Royal 2023
P. Royal, *Building Modern Business Applications*, https://doi.org/10.1007/978-1-4842-8992-1_11

a given piece of data. The event's sequence number can be used in a similar fashion. In the last chapter, I mentioned passing in an asOfRevision value to mutations to support optimistic locking within the command processor. Consider where finer-grained optimistic locking is appropriate for your domain and include the revision number in your schema.

In my work, I like to create a reusable GraphQL type that contains both provenance information as well as the revision number. Unfortunately, there isn't yet a formalized DateTime scalar within GraphQL, but there is an open proposal.

Do not over-index on future-proofing the model. Consider the view model to be ephemeral. The authoritative state for our system is stored in the event log. A view model can be recreated, if necessary, a topic I discuss in more depth later in this chapter.

While the model I am primarily discussing is for GraphQL, if you have other RPC methods you need to support simultaneously, consider having multiple event materializer instances with your service, each maintaining a customized view.

Event Materializer Behavior

The behavior of the event materializer is straightforward. It consumes new events from the event log and calls a function for each one that updates a stateful view. Your view could be wholly ephemeral, maintained in memory for each one of your application instances. In practice, I believe you will end up using an external state store of some variety. After updating the view for one event, it then moves on to the next. It is *critical* that events are processed sequentially, otherwise the view's state will be corrupted.

Transactions

I *strongly* encourage using a transactional store. In the prior section, I encouraged the use of denormalization in the view model. A single event could involve updating multiple pieces of data and the callers to your system should always see consistent states. They should not be able to read partially materialized events.

It is also possible to provide an additional consistency guarantee, that the view is consistent relative to a command. In Chapter 9 where I described the command processor, I introduced a side channel of data, the processed command log. The processed command log contains an event for each command that has a pointer to the most recent event that the processing of the command created. This knowledge can be used to window the event log into batches that correspond to the commands that yielded each batch. Each batch is then a transactional boundary for the event materializer. This ensures that reads into the system always encounter states that are consistent at the end of each mutation.

Consistency

The event materializer is maintaining a stateful view. If the system were to restart, it needs to store metadata about the last materialized event, otherwise it would reprocess events and corrupt the view. This state should be stored as an additional structure within your view. I used the term *checkpoints* to refer to this state. The checkpoints will contain the most recently materialized event sequence number, updated transactionally as events are materialized. When the system restarts it will use this sequence number to know where to restart consumption of the event log.

The checkpoints can also be used to provide read-after-write consistency for mutations. In Chapter 10 I described how successful mutations only yield a single value, the sequence number of the final event. This sequence number can then be an optional argument for GraphQL queries to indicate that the event materializer must have materialized at least this event.

It is important to note that this is only for callers that have made a mutation. They are the only ones with knowledge that the system state has changed, and thus they are the only ones that know they should wait for the system to perform an action. This behavior is eventual consistency, a topic I discussed in Chapter 6 when talking about time. If a mutation and a query from two different callers arrive shortly after one another, the query isn't guaranteed to see the results of the mutation, as it could still be working its way through the command processor and event materializer. If the two callers are working together, it will be their responsibility to share the mutator's visibleAsOfRevision with the querier. This is extra work, but at the same time it is work that makes explicit the coupling between these two callers. I believe in the longer term the dependencies in the composed system are better exposed, aiding in maintainability. If this is a bristling realization, consider how it could be architecturally eliminated from the callers.

Multiple Sources

While the primary input to the event materializer will be our system's event log, sometimes it is necessary to use data from other systems when computing derived data.

In Chapter 9, when describing the command processing engine, I mentioned that a generalization of our event log would be a message log. The event materializer doesn't need to be limited by consuming our system's event log. It can be generalized to consume from any message log.

A class of business rules involves display logic, something I introduced in Chapter 5. If the display logic requires information from another system, if the data from the other system can be presented as a message log, it can be straightforward to incorporate with our event materializer. This is also aligned with a property of reactive systems, being message driven.

An event materializer with a single event log source has a loop of:

1. Take the next event from the event log.

2. Call a materialization function with the event to update a stateful view.

3. Update the checkpoints with the event's sequence number.

4. Go to step one.

To generalize this to support multiple sources, a mechanism is needed to know which event log an event originated from so that a checkpoint for each source can be maintained. In order to retain the sequential nature of the event materializer, all the event logs it is consuming from should be merged. From the perspective of the event materializer, the stream of events it will materialize can be partitioned by the originating event log. A reasonable name in this context would be to consider each event log to be a **partition** to the event materializer. Prior to entering the event materializer, each event should be augmented to contain the partition it originated from. This information will then be used by the checkpointing component to track a per-partition checkpoint. When the system restarts, the checkpoint for each partition can correctly resume consumption of each event log.

When merging multiple event logs, events will be interleaved based upon their arrival time. Our display logic code that is maintaining the stateful view needs to arrive at the same result independent of the arrival order.

The maintenance of this derived data at materialization time, compared to request, also increases both the responsiveness and the resiliency of our system. Our system is more responsive because the time it takes to do the data derivation happens once at event materialization time, rather than being a part of the time to service a request. By consuming external data at event materialization time, we also remove the variability in response time from the external system from our system's response time. Our system's resilience is also increased. A failure to communicate with the other system doesn't impact the ability of our system to service read requests. It also doesn't impact the event materialization process as it will manifest as a period of quiescence in receiving new events.

I find this pattern of consuming data from external systems to be extremely powerful. My ideal would be to have a set of systems all implemented as ours. The message log representing the external system could be a GraphQL subscription, a mechanism I discuss later in this chapter, announcing changes to the stateful view of that system. It could be a version of that system's event log, ideally one that has mapped events into a format that is durable as a contract between the systems.

It is also possible to use this paradigm to integrate with request/response style systems. The implementation of an external event log could be making requests to the other system behind the scenes, presenting its results as an event log. Again, this is a resilient way of integration as communication latencies and failures don't impact the event materializer.

Evolving the View Model

Earlier in this chapter, I introduced the idea of having multiple event materializers to maintain different views for different consumers. This same idea can also be extended to support evolution of a single view. Recall that the view model should be considered ephemeral as the authoritative store of state is the event log. This means that breaking schema changes are not a restriction of our system. The event materializer can be "rewound" to consume from the start of the event log, fully rebuilding the view.

When I introduced the reactive principles in Chapter 4, for resiliency, I mentioned how deployments would always put your system into a temporary unexpected state. There will either be fewer instances running than desired, if you stop all the old instances before starting the new ones, or more, if you start the new ones and stop the old ones when they are able to handle requests.

It is this latter state, having more instances running, that is akin to having multiple event materializers. The materializers from the old and new versions could be running simultaneously! A new version of code that contains backward-incompatible view model changes can store its stateful view into a new location. This brings multiple benefits. First, the old version of the code can continue to service requests while the new code is rebuilding the view. Second, should there be an unexpected problem with the new code, the deployment can be safely rolled back as the view used by the prior code remains untouched.

To safely use this technique, it is critical to separate changes that involve the addition of new events from breaking view model changes. Should the new codebase process commands that yield events that the old system isn't capable of handling, a rollback won't be possible.

In the mutate-in-place status quo systems I described in Chapter 2, backward-incompatible schema changes can be very tricky to manage. Removing a column from a table is not a reversible operation; it will be necessary to restore the database itself from a backup. Experienced developers will shy away from backward-incompatible changes as the experience of dealing with one gone awry provides the lived experience of how risk-prone they can be. Even reversible changes, such as changing the data type of a column, can be tricky to manage. Database schema management is frequently integrated with an application's codebase. When the system starts, it performs any necessary forward migrations. If the code is rolled back, the old version of the code doesn't have knowledge of how to undo the changes that a newer version made. This adds a separate process to run any rollback scripts to reverse the migrations. A risk of having a separate process is that it is one that is unlikely to be done frequently, adding additional risk to performing it correctly under the likely duress of needing to roll back a change. This is ultimately an additional argument as to why build business applications as reactive systems, and in the manner I describe. The constructs and practices that I've described steer developers toward practices that reduce risk.

Communicating Changes to Others

Business applications do not exist in isolation. While they act as sources of truth for the information they manage, the applications also need to collaborate with others. This could be collaboration with humans via the applications user interface, or collaboration with other software systems. In either case, the system should be able to be *proactive* in communicating changes. The architecture I have laid out describes a system that is able to understand when its data has changed. This has been toward the goal of effectively communicating those changes to others. There are two broad categories to this communication. The first is the communication of state changes within the system to whomever it may be useful. The second is a class of business rules, side effects, that explicitly involve state changes in systems other than our own.

GraphQL Subscriptions

One of our system's self-imposed constraints from Chapter 7 is the ability to support a real-time user interface. This constraint exists because I believe it is important to bring this capability to business applications to meet user expectations of how software systems behave. The event materializer maintains a stateful view for the system's GraphQL endpoint. After each materialized event, there is an opportunity to communicate what has changed.

GraphQL subscriptions are a general mechanism for transmitting events. The GraphQL specification does not define any semantics for a subscription stream, other than it is a sequence of the field's return type.

The pattern I like to use is known as the *live query* pattern. There have been off-and-on discussions within the GraphQL community about formalizing this pattern using a directive, @live, on queries. The result will be the same as what I am describing.

I design my GraphQL schemas so that the types between subscriptions and queries are shared as follows:

```
type Customer {
    id: ID!
    name: String
}

type Query {
    customerById(id: ID!): Customer
}

type Subscription {
    customerById(id: ID!): Customer
}
```

This small snippet of a GraphQL schema defines a `Customer` type and a query to access a state snapshot, `customerById`. It also defines a subscription field with the same name, reusing the same type.

The query behavior is straightforward GraphQL; requesting the query field will yield the current state of the customer in a single response. Unfortunately, a GraphQL schema doesn't contain information to define the semantics of a subscription (which is part of the rationale for the `@live` directive). For subscriptions implementing the live query pattern, upon subscription callers will receive a snapshot of the current state. As changes are made to the requested data, additional snapshots will be sent. The subscription is infinite; if results for the query exist, the subscription will continue to tick as query results change.

Conceptually, our system's stream of events, representing changes, are materialized into a stateful view by the event materializer. As changes to this stateful view are made, subscriptions allow for the observation of those changes in the form of a series of states.

I have found this communication paradigm to work well with user interfaces. UIs are often displaying full states and communicating the full state on each underlying change simplifies their implementation. As an implementation note, the semantics of communicating full states with each subscription tick does not mean that the underlying transport needs to send the full state with each tick. Subscriptions are stateful, so an implementation could optimize for the network layer by only communicating the difference between ticks. This optimization can exist at the transport layer, providing the illusion for developers that the full state is communicated each time.

The use of subscriptions isn't limited to UIs. There may be other collaborating systems that need to use the state of our system. They too can use a GraphQL subscription to access the changes from our system. This works best when the collaborating system only needs to be aware of the state change and isn't concerned with *why* there was a state change. If collaborating systems need to know why, the interaction may be better thought of as a side effect from our system. If possible, using the same mechanism for a UI as well as collaborating systems helps limit the number of external contracts our system has. There is a balance to strike here. As developers, limiting the number of external contracts reduces the work required when changes are made. In tension with this is the need to coordinate with a larger number of parties when changes are made. There is no right answer as to where the balance lies. I believe the important part is to have the decision be an intentional one.

After each materialized event, you can use the information contained within the event to determine the set of impacted GraphQL subscriptions. This may also be functionality that your choice of datastore for the stateful view provides. As the stateful view is updated, it can either generate or facilitate the propagation of, change events that our system consumes and uses to power GraphQL subscriptions.

Other Side Effects

In addition to notifying users and collaborating systems about changes to our system's state, there may be business processes that our system is a part of. In Chapter 5, when introducing how I think about business rules, I described a class of rule I termed *side effects*. Side effects can be further broken down into two categories: those that depend upon the view state and those that don't. For the side effects that don't depend upon the view state directly, consider whether there is an indirect dependency for you, the developer. If something unexpected occurs in the system and you need to investigate, would ensuring that side effects happen after event materialization aid in potential future debugging efforts? Perhaps not, but I always encourage this line of thinking when designing systems. Your future self may thank you.

An example of a side effect that would depend upon the view would be the maintenance of another derivative data store. The stateful store that we use to store our view may be efficient for direct lookup by identifiers but may not efficiently offer some other desired product features, such as full text or faceted search. There may be another store that is able to answer these queries more efficiently and for operational simplicity the store is loaded with the results of GraphQL queries from our service. Yes, you could have an additional event materializer that maintains state within this store, but there is a trade-off between the code duplication of the two stores vs. having one be a derivative of the other.

This type of side effect could operate by following the system's event log, but then delaying the handling of each event until the event materializer has successfully materialized a given event. As the side effect handles each event, it can reuse the same checkpointing mechanism as the event materializer. Its progress can be stored as an additional partition within the event materializer's checkpoints. An important detail here is that if the view is recreated, the side effects will occur again, as the state that is stored within the view will be lost. For the example at hand, updating a derivative data store based on our view, this is desired. For the other category, participation in business processes, this will be undesirable.

A side effect that is a part of a business process, such as sending approved payments to a bank, or sending new customers a welcome email, should not be redone when the view is recreated. They will need a checkpointing mechanism akin to what the event materializer uses, but one that is durable. It is feasible to reuse the command processor itself for this state keeping by modeling both the intent to perform an action as well as the action's disposition as command and events. With whichever route is chosen, and discrete from the ideas around business applications in this book, the action should be idempotent. The information within our system, such as the event log sequence number, can assist in constructing an idempotency token that the next step in the business process can use to determine if there is an attempt to perform an action an additional time. Failures will happen and actions will be retried. While having a customer receive a second welcome email may be acceptable, sending payments more than once is not.

Managing Failure

Failure will happen, whether planned or not. The event materializer is maintaining a stateful view, which likely means an external system is managing the state keeping. This external system will not be available 100% of the time, as at a minimum it is likely to require software updates. Unexpected failures can always happen as well, such as a bug in the event materializer in handling a given event. It is necessary to explicitly plan for failure, rather than thinking of ourselves as perfect developers that won't write bugs and thinking that unplanned failures are sufficiently unlikely. Our systems are important to the business, which is why we are writing them in the first place.

If the stateful view store itself is unavailable, that impacts the ability to read from our system. However, notably, the system will continue to accept writes. The command processor is decoupled from the event materializer, and a failure in the event materializer doesn't halt command processing. Depending upon the places where optimistic locking is used, writes may become effectively disabled though, as without a way to observe what the latest sequence number is, callers will be unable to read the value in order to provide it to mutations.

The event materializer is sequentially consuming from the event log. If there is a failure in handling an event, the event materializer **must** stop. If the event materializer were to try and "skip" an event, its view will be inconsistent. However, the entire event materializer doesn't need to stop. If the event materializer is processing multiple input partitions, a failure handling an event only needs to stop that partition, not the entire materializer (although you may find the policy of stopping the entire materializer easier to implement initially).

This behavior is likely to be undesirable to some when it is explained. You may be encouraged to couple command processing and event materialization into a single unit of work that can either succeed or fail in unison. I caution against this, as I believe it is an attempt to bend the system's architecture to one's development practices. The risk that others will have in mind relates to programming errors, not view store failures, as this coupling doesn't change behavior in the event of a view store failure. I believe that, and have found in practice, that testing can sufficiently mitigate this risk, the subject of the next section. There can still be gaps in tests, and my fallback is then development practices that are largely out of scope for this book. By having a fast build process and practicing continuous delivery, you should ideally be able to take changes you've made into production in a timely fashion. You can use the duration of these processes as the minimum amount of time it will take to get any code changes deployed. This is a starting point for conversations with your business partners to understand what the system's availability objectives are, which can guide implementation decisions. When the event materializer fails to handle an event due to programming errors, it doesn't impact the system's ability to service read requests. The ability to have partial failures such as this is a form of resiliency.

Testing

The event materializer is deterministic. Given an input event, it should perform the same action each time. This is should, not will, as there is the possibility that the action could vary: when the event materializer is consuming from multiple input partitions. Determinism remains, but the number of possible actions is a function of the number of partitions. In the simple case of having two partitions with events A and B, it is necessary to handle A then B, as well as B then A. This also depends upon your implementation though. The handling of A and B could be independent, with a common routine that is executed after A or B has been handled. In much of my work, the testing of how the event materializer handles an event isn't performed as testing of the event materializer, it is performed as testing of the entire system. In order to test how the event materializer has handled an event, it will be necessary to query the stateful view. This is related to the testing of GraphQL queries and subscriptions against this view. I've found that testing the entire system is preferable, for reasons that I'll explain in depth in the next chapter.

The stateful view model is also an opportunity to check the results of the command processor. If the stateful view is stored in a system that allows for declarative constraints, such as a relational database, the capabilities of the store can be used. I have found it beneficial to cross-check both unique constraints as well as foreign key relationships. Should handling of an event violate a constraint, it will point to an error within the command processor, not the event materializer. This is an example of the type of error that should be caught within tests, as should this occur within a deployed system, the remediation would require the removal of the view constraint, and then handling the fix as a business rule change as described in Chapter 6.

While testing the entire system makes sense for how the event materializer handles any given event, the event materializer itself can, and should, be tested in isolation. When testing the entire system, it is important to minimize the possibility that those tests fail due to errors in the event materializer itself. The isolated tests for the event materializer should be written against a set of events that are unrelated to your domain and ridiculously simple. I use simple domains, and like the command generator tests, often silly ones that personalize the tests, such as counting the number of times my cat has been fed.

Testing the event materializer in isolation also makes the simulation of failures more straightforward. Tests can be written to simulate the failure of the stateful view store, as well as guards around soft handler failures such as failing to complete within a given timeframe.

Summary

The event materializer maintains the stateful view model that is used to satisfy GraphQL queries and subscriptions. You have learned how this model can evolve over time, and how the evolution of the view model is akin to maintaining multiple purpose-built view models. I have explained how the view is best maintained transactionally, and how the command processor's processed command log can be used to provide consistency of the view relative to a command. You have learned how to think about testing the event materializer, what testing is appropriate for the materializer itself, and what testing is best done on the entire system, the topic of the next chapter.

CHAPTER 12

Testing, Monitoring, and Observability

The prior three chapters introduced our system's key components: the Command Processor, Command Generator, and Event Materializer. Each of those chapters contained a section relating to how to test the component. The testing of each component in isolation builds confidence in the component itself. That doesn't translate to confidence in the composed system. It is necessary to test all components working together, end-to-end. In this chapter, you will learn how I've approached testing to build this confidence. I discuss the value of being able to understand the internal state of the system from its outputs and how to instrument our system to achieve this. You will learn why it is necessary to consider how the system will be operated in production during the design phase. Let's go.

Key Components

Before discussing how to test the system's major components end-to-end, I wanted to refresh ourselves on the components and how they are tested in isolation.

Command Processor

The command processor is responsible for maintaining a class of business rules, the rules for data at rest. As input, it takes a command, which is a request to change the state of the system. A function you provide, the mutator, is provided with a command and the current system state and is responsible for generating a set of events that describes the changes the command wishes to enact. Another function you provide, the applicator, takes in an event and the system state, returning a new state instance that incorporates the changes the event describes. The applicator and mutator are pure functions, functions with no side effects. The state instance is an immutable data structure containing the necessary state to enforce the business rules.

These three items, the applicator and mutator functions, plus the state, are the application-specific portions of the command processor. The remainder of the command processor's implementation is agnostic to the logic within these functions.

In Chapter 9, I described how the applicator, mutator, and state can be tested individually. They can also be orchestrated in a test without using the command processor itself.

Command Generator

The command generator is responsible for the creation of a command from a change request, such as the system's GraphQL mutations. It submits the command for processing by appending it to the command log. It is then responsible for awaiting the command's disposition and communicating that to the caller.

The testing described in Chapter 10 was around the mechanical infrastructure of this component, rather than the domain-specific work of creating a command. I deferred the testing of the domain-specific logic to this chapter.

Event Materializer

The event materializer maintains the stateful view that is used to answer GraphQL queries.

Like the command generator, I described in Chapter 11 how the event materializer itself can be tested in isolation. The checkpointing infrastructure and orchestration of the view maintenance can be tested with simple events that are divorced from your actual domain. This gives confidence that the event materializer itself works before using the materialization functions for your domain's events. Just like the command generator, I believe the domain-specific portions of the event materializer are best tested by testing the composed data flow.

Composed Data Flow

From write to read, change requests are communicated to the system as a GraphQL mutation. The command generator converts the mutation input into a command, performing any necessary communication with external systems. It submits the command to the command log, which establishes the order of execution. The command processing engine consumes commands from the command log one at a time. For each command, it calls your mutator function to create the set of events the command implies. It then calls your application function to advance the command processor's state. If both items succeed, the events are appended to the event log, and a processed command is recorded with the disposition of the command.

The command generator is awaiting this disposition. If the command fails, a detailed error is returned. Otherwise, the sequence number of the final event the command generated is returned.

The event materializer is consuming from the event log. As soon as the events are appended, it will start updating the stateful view. This happens in parallel with the communication of the command disposition to callers, only for successful commands of course, as a failed command would yield no events.

To observe their changes, the caller can execute a GraphQL query, providing the sequence number from the mutation response as an indicator of the minimum view version they require. This provides read-after-write consistency for callers that make changes. Callers can also use an active GraphQL subscription to observe the change. They will receive a subscription tick after the event materializer has updated the view.

To test the system in a way that gives confidence that it will handle requests from callers, it is necessary to exercise this composed data flow.

Testing the Composed System

I think tests for a system (or service) aren't fully appreciated. In the past several years the idea of a "test pyramid" has been spreading, originating from Mike Cohn's book *Succeeding with Agile*.[1] The body of the pyramid is composed of comparatively more isolated and faster unit tests. The top of the pyramid is more integrated and slower UI tests. The middle is comprised of service (or system) tests. When done well, systems

---

[1] ISBN 9780321660534

tests can provide high levels of confidence in a system and be performant. With a mix of using containers, the ease of running tests on cloud-based machines, or even remote development environments, the speed penalty is evaporating. I also believe there is sometimes the perception that any tests more complex than unit tests are slow and expensive.

My approach for system tests is to test what is valuable. I value system's external API contracts, in our case the GraphQL schema, as well as any infrastructure used to satisfy the API contracts. The event materializer maintains a stateful view. If another system is used to store the view (e.g., a database), then the tests should use an actual instance of that system. Containers have greatly helped here as they provide a normalized contract for managing the lifecycle of this class of resource.

GraphQL is often delivered using HTTP. For system tests, I avoid this, preferring to interface with my GraphQL implementation directly. The interface between a GraphQL implementation and the HTTP endpoint exposing it is testable in isolation. This is the same philosophy applied to the event materializer tests. The component is providing functionality that is ultimately agnostic as to what operation it is performing. The event materializer isn't concerned with how any given event affects the stateful view. The interface between the HTTP endpoint and the GraphQL implementation is similar, and because it exists as the edge of the system, easily bypassed.

I believe the composed system, everything necessary to satisfy the GraphQL API can be tested as a whole; a single *unit*, if you need to phrase the argument in that nomenclature. Our system needs to uphold its external contracts, and testing from a similar vantage point as the system's users provides greater confidence that the test results will be reflective of how the system behaves in production.

A corollary of testing our system from the perspective of external contracts is that the same can be applied to any systems that ours needs to collaborate with. If the command generator needs to interrogate another system in order to create a command, a stub implementation of that other system can be used in our tests provided it satisfies the other system's contract. I find this perspective also avoids the creation of a distributed monolith, the requirement to release multiple services in lockstep due to their interdependencies. If contracts between systems are underspecified, perhaps even to the point of not existing, developers can lean toward using live instances of collaborating systems for tests. A well-specified contract allows for the creation of alternate implementations, a contributing factor in avoiding this type of coupling within tests.

For our system, an implementation should allow the instantiation of the GraphQL interface, command generator, command processor, event materializer, and any additional required services. It is the essence of the entire system, ready to be exposed via HTTP when deployed.

This instance of the composed system is sufficient to test the composed data flow. The type of tests are also ones from an under-appreciated paradigm, property-based testing.

Introducing Property-Based Testing

When explaining property-based testing to colleagues, I first root their understanding in what they know. Most developers are familiar with tests that take the following form:

```
@Test
void shouldCalculateScore() {
    var customer = new TestCustomer();
    var calculator = new ScoreCalculator();
    assertEquals(10, calculator.scoreFor(customer));
}
```

This type of test is an example-based test. The rationale for the name is straightforward, the test is asserting the score for a specifically created customer. Consider how I have just provided you with an example of a familiar test.

It can be hard to create general assertions about the behavior of the score calculator. How much of the implementation is exercised by that one test customer?

Developers will often use their knowledge of the implementation to craft multiple examples to exercise different code paths in the implementation. Together, these examples build confidence that the tests provide confidence to the system's behavior when deployed.

There is a limitation with this approach; as complexity in the inputs to the unit under test increases, so must the number of examples. I have found that this does not integrate nicely with the desires of most developers to minimize the volume of code they need to author, especially when the code is highly repetitive. There are techniques that test frameworks offer to help minimize repetition, but ultimately if you have 100 examples, you will have at least 100 of *something* within the codebase.

It is this that led me to property-based testing. The premise is straightforward: rather than testing specific examples of inputs and outputs, test the properties of the unit for all possible inputs. In practice, testing all possible inputs is often infeasible. Frameworks that support property-based testing will instead start with a random seed value and use that to generate a set of inputs. Should one of the inputs fail the random seed value can be provided to the framework to reproduce the scenario for developers to fix.

Literature on property-based testing often uses symmetric functions in their examples. For any object A, if it is serialized to an external representation and deserialized again, it should equal the original value. Mathematically, this would be written as `A = deserialize(serialize(A))`.

The approach I find powerful is the usage of a *test oracle*. A test oracle is a component that can provide the expected output for a given input without knowledge of how the non-test oracle is implemented. If your initial reaction is that this requires a second implementation of a unit's logic, you are correct!

When using property-based testing combined with a test oracle that can provide the expected output for a given input, you are writing a second implementation of the unit's logic. I believe this is a good thing. To be an effective oracle, it must not depend on the implementation that is under test. It is a wholly separate implementation. Since it is code that is only used for testing, it does not need to be as resilient as code that runs in production. It can be simplified for the task at hand.

Consider this a developer's version of double-entry bookkeeping. Just as accountants use two ledgers to ensure correctness of their books, as developers we can have two implementations of our business logic. By implementing business logic twice, each one independent, they act as a cross-check for each other. The implementations will help you ensure that the other is doing what it is intended to do.

Once a test oracle has been created, reuse is extremely low-cost. The maintenance of 10's, much less 100's, of example-based test cases will become cumbersome. A property-based test can be run with 1000's of randomly generated inputs (or, for inputs that are from an enumerable finite set, all possible inputs). The limiting factor will be the balance between test runtime and the increased confidence from additional inputs; one that you can tune for your environment and risk tolerance.

When property-based testing frameworks generate inputs, they will often have hooks for generating special values. Special values are the type of values that can cause edge cases, such as zeros, null values, or the minimum and maximum values for signed numbers. These hooks for special values ensure that they are incorporated into randomly generated inputs with greater probability.

The ability to test business logic with more scenarios than I would want to manually manage is extremely powerful in building confidence in a system. The next section explains how to do this for our system.

Using Property-Based Testing

We will use property-based testing to validate our system's behavior relative to the exposed GraphQL interface. At the most basic level, after executing a GraphQL mutation, validate that the queries and subscriptions contain the expected changes. Testing a single mutation at a time is unlikely to build the desired confidence. User workflows likely span multiple mutations. Consider a system that manages invoices. There may be mutations to:

- Create an invoice

- Submit an invoice for approval

- Approve an invoice

- Reject an invoice

- Archive an invoice

After creation, invoices may be approved or rejected. Rejected invoices can be reapproved. Only rejected invoices may be archived.

What we really want is to have our property-based test not only generate the inputs for creating an invoice, but to also generate the sequence of actions to take.

This technique gets powerful. What if there is an implementation edge case where archival fails after an invoice has been submitted for approval multiple times? Is that scenario one that you may have written as an example-based test? I suspect I would have written a test that verifies the archival of a rejected invoice, not considering that the number of rejections may be a trigger for failure.

By having the property-based test framework generate a series of actions to perform, we can simulate the various paths through a system's workflows that users may take. In my own work this has uncovered subtle edge cases in unexpected sequences that would have been far more difficult to piece together from a user's support request.

In order to support testing a series of actions, the property-based tests for our system need to be backed by a stateful test oracle. When an action is performed, the mutation is sent to the system, as well as the test oracle. The changes the mutation implied will be visible in GraphQL queries and subscriptions, and the oracle will be consulted to predict what the values will be.

When writing property-based tests and their associated oracle, it is critical that all actions are deterministic. This allows for the replay of a test scenario should an expectation fail. As an example, one pitfall that I've encountered is having the test oracle store state using a Java `HashMap`. Java's `HashMap` does not guarantee an iteration order of its contents, something you may rely on in a test to get an "nth" entry from the map. The fix is straightforward, use a `LinkedHashMap` instead as it does provide the desired guarantee.

The system itself also needs to be deterministic, but we have already largely guaranteed that in the design itself. Mutations are handled by the command generator, which ultimately appends a command to the command log. The order of commands within the command log defines the order that they will be processed in. In the face of concurrent mutations, this is where order is established. After the command generator, all processing is ordered, whether it is consuming from the command log in the command processor, appending to the event log, or consuming from the event log in the event materializer. The tests can execute mutations sequentially, knowing that they will be generating the possible orders that could be seen when deployed due to concurrent requests.

The design itself is deterministic. What may not be is any work that is done within the command generator that consults external systems in order to create commands. You will need to solve this for your system, and the solution will vary based upon what the work is. A possibility is to treat the response from the external system as another input to the action that requires it. When the test executes the action, it can use a side channel to communicate to the stub implementation, telling it what its next response should be.

In practice, I use property-based tests to validate what I *think* is the happy path through the system. The generated series of actions to take is *expected* to always result in successful mutations. My reasons are two-fold. First, I don't care about the full universe of invalid values. If the creation of an invoice has a constraint that the invoice date can't be in the past, is there value in testing all possible past dates? Personally, I don't gain additional confidence in the system by doing so. I am happy to rely on my knowledge of how the check is implemented. Second, more practically, it simplifies the test and oracle implementations. The generated inputs are constrained to match the system's rules and the oracle doesn't need to be able to predict errors. If a mutation from the property-based test of the system fails, the diagnosis is straightforward. The generation of the input values wasn't properly constrained, which should be straightforwardly visible from the error message, or the test found a genuine problem in the system.

An additional benefit of testing at this level is the ability to evolve the internals of the system. With the tests anchored to the system's external contracts, there is more freedom to evolve the internals of the system. You can ensure that internal system changes that should have no external impact don't have one by cross-checking your changes with an absence of changes to the tests.

Property-based testing is powerful, but it isn't a panacea for all testing needs.

Using Example Tests

In the prior section, I described how I constrain property-based tests to generate inputs and actions that are expected to succeed, the happy path. These tests validate the state changes from mutations as visible from GraphQL queries and subscriptions.

Callers of our system won't stick to the happy path. The system will certainly receive inputs that will violate the system's business rules. When that inevitably occurs, the reasons for violation should be communicated so the caller is able to determine their next course of action.

This is where I find value in example tests. Example tests can be used to ensure that the system rejects invalid inputs or actions. The validation that example tests perform should not only include the fact that a mutation was rejected, but also the returned information about *why* it failed. For callers to determine their next course of action, the reason for failure needs to be clearly communicated to them. Assertions within example tests should ensure that error messages are sufficiently descriptive.

Example tests are also useful early in the life of the system. When the very first mutation is being added, and its results are being checked against the view, using an example test for this is the most straightforward approach to validate this work. Even for a multistep workflow such as the invoice approval example, writing it out as an example test initially helps me get early feedback on the implementation. Once I have the example working, I will either start or enhance the property-based test of the system.

When a test expectation fails, you will need to understand why. It could be the inputs are invalid, or there is a logic error within the system. Encountering logic errors early in the development process is preferred, but not always possible. Once the system is running in a deployed environment, debugging won't be as straightforward as during development. Often, I will aim to recreate the scenario that is causing an error as an example test. To effectively do so, I may need to know some of the internal states of the system.

Observability

Observability is a term from control theory that describes the measure of how well the internal states of a system can be inferred from the system's outputs. The more accurate the inference, the more observable the system.

For software developers, I consider this to be the ability to infer the internal state of a system by observing the requests and responses the system has received and returned, log output, and system metrics such as memory consumed or CPU usage.

Requests, responses, logs, and metrics are all correlatable. In the simplest case, time can be used. This starts to become more difficult when there are concurrent requests to a system, additional metadata needs to be included on every log statement to indicate what request it corresponds to. System metrics are aggregations, there's no breakdown of exactly how much memory or CPU a given request may be consuming.

A solution to this is tracing. You may have heard of tracing in the context of distributed tracing, tracking how requests flow within a distributed system. In the commonly used nomenclature, a single request is a *trace*. A trace is composed of a unique ID and multiple spans, a container for tracking a duration. Each span has a start time and a duration, a *timespan*. Spans are organized into a tree, so it is possible to visualize dependencies. If service A calls service B as a part of handling a request, there will be a span representing the call to service B that would be a descendant of the span that represents the call to service A.

As a metaphor, tracing is akin to delivery tracking. Consider a package that a friend sends you via the postal system. Your friend receives a tracking number when they drop off the package. This is akin to a trace's unique ID. As the package is handled by the various facilities on its journey to you, there will be timestamped entries for each. Ultimately, the package arrives on your doorstep.

Tracing provides the model to achieve this type of visibility in computer systems, and we can apply it to the internals of our system. The tracing model is extremely useful, even if it is not a part of a larger distributed system. Each request into our system is at least one span that represents the external view of the request, including the duration. Each of the key components in our system is a discrete step. The tracing model allows for the creation of a span to represent the work performed in each, as well as the linking of them together. For a mutation, the trace would contain a span for the entire request, and then have descendants representing the command generator, command processor, and event materializer. Even though the caller will receive a result after the command processor has completed, the work of the event materializer should be a part of the trace since it is related.

Callers will have knowledge of a trace's unique ID. When using distributed tracing, there are mechanisms for propagating this contextual information with requests, or if the system is using tracing in isolation, the value can be returned as part of the response. If the request resulted in an error or was unexpectedly slow, the trace can be interrogated to gain additional insight. This contributes to the system being observable, as the trace is another output of the system. We can use the trace to build a more complete mental model of the system's internal state. The envelope pattern I mentioned in Chapter 10 with the command generator can also be used to track the trace associated with the envelope's contents.

As you implement the components of our system, consider where you may add additional spans to capture interesting pieces of work. Be liberal in adding spans when writing code. I view it as the software equivalent of running cables in a building that is under construction prior to closing the walls. It is both simpler and more cost-efficient to do it early in the building process rather than needing to retrofit existing work.

Tracing is commoditized and there are existing solutions for your chosen language that you can build upon. A common feature is the ability to add arbitrary key-value pairs to each span, often referred to as tags. I encourage you to also be extremely liberal here, adding as much contextual information as you have available at the time. It is hard to predict what may be useful in the future.

There are vendors you can send your traces to that allow you to perform analytics upon them. Each span is equivalent to a timer as it contains a start time and a duration. By instrumenting your code with a trace, it eliminates the need to separately capture timing information as a metric. Tracing is also more powerful. Metrics are pre-aggregated, so a timer surrounding a piece of code would at best record a histogram of its observed durations. If you then look at the timer values and see a slow outlier, you can't tie it back to the specific request that was slow. By using traces as the input, a timer can be derived by aggregating the spans of the trace. If a slow outlier is observed, the input traces can be queried to understand exactly what the outliers were doing. This is also where adding tags beforehand becomes valuable, as tooling can also use the tags as additional dimensions for querying.

Traces have become my preferred method for observing deployed systems. If there is a support request related to unexpected behavior, if I am provided with the trace ID related to the interaction, I can understand exactly what the inputs were and how the system behaved.

Metrics such as CPU and memory usage do have their place. System-wide values that describe the overall behavior of the system and its host environment are valuable and should still be collected. It is beneficial to understand the aggregate behavior of the system, and not all the necessary data can be constructed from traces.

Traces are also useful with property-based testing. Each arbitrarily chosen action can start a new trace, allowing for the mutation execution and any queries used for verification to be represented as their own spans. If you can confidently use traces to debug test failures, you will be more confident about using traces to diagnose behavior when the system is deployed. Using traces to debug test failures is also an early opportunity to understand what the valuable contextual tags for your domain are.

While traces provide a mechanism to monitor the system, I prefer to refer to them as an observability tool, something to understand what the system is doing. Monitoring is a separate activity that could use traces to achieve other goals.

Monitoring Production Systems

I consider monitoring to be the act of ensuring that the system is doing what it is supposed to be doing. Monitoring will be accompanied by some form of alerting, as the system's operators, that is, you, will want to know when the system isn't doing what it should be.

The system described in this book is amenable to a single process to ensure overall health. I find this beneficial as sometimes systems will have many monitoring processes generating alerts. When a system has many alerts, there is the increased likelihood of a misfire, or you will receive a deluge of alerts when there is a problem, requiring you to determine which one points at the actual problem.

For a business application, the ideal monitoring mechanism would be to perform the same actions as the system's callers. Unfortunately, for business applications, having a monitoring system make changes to the system's data will be undesirable to the business.

Another approach can be used with our system. What we ultimately want to know is whether commands are being processed, events are being materialized, and queries are being answered. This can be achieved by using a mutation that doesn't impact the system's business information. A mutation can be added to increment a counter. The counter will generate a command, and the processing of generating this command will yield an event. The event materializer will materialize the event, updating a stored value in the view. A GraphQL query and/or subscription can be used to observe the updated value.

If this process is completing in a timely manner, other mutations and queries to the system should also complete (if there aren't any logic errors). The time it takes this process to complete is also a health indicator of how responsive the system is. If the time starts to slow, an alert can be generated to give an early warning of potential performance problems.

This type of process is referred to as synthetic monitoring, as we are simulating the actions a user may take. We are leveraging the fact that all mutations flow through the same process to avoid the need to change any business information while gaining confidence that the processes would be able to handle any actual requests to change business information.

I find that synthetic monitoring works extremely well with property-based testing. Property-based tests provide confidence that the logic within the system behaves as expected. The synthetic monitoring is verifying that materials are flowing through the system's metaphorical pipes. This is again the same paradigm that was used for testing the event materializer, the separation of testing the infrastructure from the business logic. If the infrastructure itself can be verified, there is confidence that it will work for whatever business logic is relying upon the infrastructure.

When the system's monitor fires an alert, the first course of action will be to reach for the tools you have available to diagnose the system, such as the system where you can interrogate traces or view system metrics.

Practice Using Tools

Writing tests is beneficial to ensure that your system will do what it is expected to do. Monitoring is beneficial to ensure that the system is operational and responding to requests. When the monitor eventually triggers an alert, or a caller reports an error that they've received, you will need to rely on your tools to diagnose the problem.

Learning to use the tools you have available to diagnose problems *while trying to diagnose a problem* is an exercise in frustration, not to mention either lengthening the diagnosis time or an inability to find the problem.

Ideally, you will know how to use the tools and interpret their data. This must be learned, and it should be done explicitly.

In my current role, we run a weekly rotation of whose turn it is to be the first responder for problems in the system. Often, there may not be any problems during the week, leading to a very straightforward hand-off process. If there have been problems, there will be a discussion to share the learned context with the individual taking responsibility.

To learn our tools and how to interpret their data, the individual who was responsible the prior week would walk the team through our tools to understand how to use them. This solves multiple goals.

Firstly, it creates what I call an *ambient understanding* of the system's behavior. By looking at the system's high-level metrics such as CPU or memory usage, you will build an understanding of what normal for your system looks like. Perhaps there is a repeating pattern of CPU usage day-over-day. You may learn that a small spike at a given time isn't out of the ordinary. Then, when triaging a problem in the system, you then know that the same small spike is unlikely to be a factor in the problem as it is a regular occurrence. If you hadn't built this ambient understanding of normal, you may end up spending time investigating something that turned out to be a red herring.

Secondly, it is an opportunity to dig into potential red herrings! Using the same small CPU spike example, the first time it is observed, dig in to understand why! Do the same type of diagnosis that would be done when triaging an actual problem, but without the pressure that real problems bring. This is where you and your team will learn how to use the tools to answer questions about the system. Perhaps the CPU spike is correlated with a latency spike. You can then look at the traces to see what requests the system was receiving. If the traces aren't providing sufficient data, you have an opportunity to enhance the captured data.

Learning how to use your tools in the middle of an incident will be frustrating. Realizing that your system isn't emitting sufficient information for you to understand its behavior will delay your ability to diagnose problems. In order to provide a resilient system, it is important for its operators, you, to learn how to operate it. Practice is required, and practice is best done in a controlled environment, not during the more stressful environment of an incident.

Testing will help minimize incidents, but it is impossible to eliminate the unexpected.

Summary

While individual components of the system can be tested in isolation, and there is value in doing so, there is also value in testing the composed system. You have learned about property-based testing and how to apply it to our system. You have also learned that there is a place for example tests, especially early on in development and to test the system's error messages. I explained the value of using traces to understand the system's internal behavior and how synthetic monitoring can be used to check that the system is operating as expected when deployed. Finally, I explained a valuable practice, to practice investigating the system to build an ambient understanding of its behavior and to ensure that it is emitting sufficient information to diagnose problems. The next chapter will review our system against our goals and look forward to what technologies are needed for an implementation.

CHAPTER 13

Required Technologies

This chapter is the culmination of my proposed design for business applications. It begins with a brief review of the system's design and then a recap of our constraints and principles, discussing how they have been incorporated.

With the full set of goals fresh in your mind, I will then go over the types of technologies that will be needed to implement the design. This will remain high level, speaking to the desired capabilities, rather than specific implementations.

At the end of this chapter, you will understand how the proposed design meets the goals and the types of building blocks you will need in order to craft an implementation. Let's dive in.

Design Review

The primary interface to the system is via GraphQL. It will provide the interface for read-only queries, real-time subscriptions, and mutating its contained data.

Starting with mutating data, the GraphQL schema contains mutations that may be invoked. Each mutation is part of a module named the command generator. The command generator is the bridge between the request/response interaction that caller's interface with and the message-driven system internals. Each mutation is backed by a function that converts the mutation's input into a command. This function may be impure, consulting external systems as needed. Commands are a type of immutable message that describe an intent to change the system's data. They are always forward looking in time and must contain all information needed to process it. After creation, the new command will be appended to the command log for further processing. The caller now has the command's sequence number and blocks further execution. It will follow the processed command log, filtering by the command's sequence number, in order to determine the command's disposition. Upon receipt of the processed command, it is mapped into a mutation result. If the command failed, that is described back to the

133

© Peter Royal 2023
P. Royal, *Building Modern Business Applications*, https://doi.org/10.1007/978-1-4842-8992-1_13

caller via appropriately descriptive types in the GraphQL schema. If the command was a success, the final generated event sequence number is returned, allowing the caller to know when changes have been incorporated into queries, or a subscription tick has been observed.

The command log is followed and consumed by the command processor. This module is responsible for translating commands into events. Events are another type of immutable message that describe something that has occurred to the system's data; they are always backward looking in time. The command processor requires two pure functions to govern its operation and interactions with immutable state. When this module starts, it will read from the event log and use one of these functions, the applicator, to derive the system's current state. The applicator takes an event and the current state and returns a new state instance that incorporates the event. This state contains the necessary information to enforce one class of business rule, the rules for data at rest. It will be a subset of all the information contained within the system. Once the current state has been derived it will be combined with a command using the mutator function to generate the set of events that describe the changes the command implies. The applicator will then be used on these events to derive the system's new state. If both functions are processed without error, the events are committed into the event log and a processed command message containing the command's sequence number, the last event's sequence number, and a success flag is committed into the processed command log. This is a transactional all-or-nothing process. If either function fails, this may represent either a programming error or a constraint violation. If the applicator failed, the events from the mutator are discarded. A processed command message is committed to the processed command log containing the command's sequence number, the sequence number of the last successfully processed event, and details about the nature of the failure.

GraphQL queries and subscriptions are handled by the view module. The specifics of this module are left unspecified as the implementation will depend upon the details of your domain. The view module accesses a materialized view of the system's data. This materialized view is maintained by the event materializer module. The event materializer consumes the event log and builds the necessary structures that will be used by the view module. There may be multiple event materializer instances if there are multiple views in use, although we have been focusing on a single instance, the one used to back the GraphQL schema. As the event materializer follows the event log it can window the stream using the processed command log. This allows the module to materialize events in batches that match command boundaries, preventing system states that are technically valid but not explicitly intended from being visible. After materializing an event the event materializer can generate a fire-and-forget event that allows the view module to generate new ticks on any active GraphQL subscriptions.

The system's design incorporates principles from both event sourcing and CQRS. The event log is the system's authoritative data store which borrows from event sourcing. Through GraphQL, commands and queries are separated, borrowing from CQRS. Mutations generate commands and flow through the system as I have described. Queries (and real-time subscriptions) are handled by the view module.

Any additional collaborating systems within your domain can be enabled with additional consumers of the event log. You will likely want to have a translation layer between the event schema that is used in the event log and the schema that is exposed to collaborators. I always recommend this to prevent tight coupling to the event log's format. This is beneficial when changes are made as it eliminates a point of coordination. The system itself can be modified and the interface exposed to collaborators can be modified on a separate cadence that works for both parties.

With the system's design fresh in your mind, the next section is a recap of our constraints and principles with a focus on how the design satisfies each of them.

Constraints and Principles Recap

There are two self-imposed constraints on the system's design, and eight guiding principles. The constraints represent strategic decisions that I believe are aligned with where the industry is heading and are synergistic with the principles. In enumerating a set of principles for the system, it is a declaration of how the system should be thought about when looking at the implementation. Decisions should tie back to one or more principles. They provide guidelines for those that may work on the system in the future. From one perspective, they are a step removed from specific architectural decisions. They are the principles by which architectural decisions are made.

GraphQL

GraphQL is a schema-driven mechanism for interfacing with a system. It has become extremely popular with UI developers due to its type system and the ability for clients to control what data is fetched. It is an open standard and is seeing active investment and adoption across the industry. GraphQL schemas can include in-line documentation for the contained types and operations as well as the ability to deprecate fields. I believe these primitives are foundational for loose coupling between systems and teams. By describing itself with a GraphQL schema, developers that need to interact with a system have the essential information available to them. There are many tools available for working with GraphQL allowing the benefits of working with schemas to be available on many platforms. Yes, there are mechanisms to achieve many of the same benefits with REST-style APIs. However, the tooling to do so isn't as rich and widely available.

GraphQL's discrete input and output types are aligned with CQRS. Mutations map to commands which drive the event-sourced architecture.

Real-Time Updates

I believe that enabling user interfaces to react in real time to changes in data is a long overdue capability for business applications. The specific ways in which this will be used will vary from application to application. Real-time updates are about enabling the proactive observation of changes to the system, whether it is used for a UI, a push notification, or an email. By adding this as a constraint to the system, it is a declaration that they are *important*. Many consumer applications have interfaces that leverage real-time updates, leading users to expect this capability in software they interact with. I believe it is time to make this capability available to business applications as well.

With the system being entirely event driven, real-time updates happen naturally. GraphQL's subscription facilities are a natural observation mechanism for these changes. When successful mutations return a sequence number indicating when the results may be observed, callers are thus steered toward using subscriptions as the primary way to interact with the system, helping enable being *real-time by default*.

Never Forget

As developers, we use source control to remember prior states of our source code. We should be providing that capability to our users for the data they manipulate without our systems. The cost of storing data continues to decline, and with cloud environments storage capacity can be added on demand. Technical reasons from the past for mutating data in place, forgetting prior states, are no longer sound. Forgetting data is a policy decision, not a technical one. Business applications should default to retaining all changes to data. This allows users to understand how data came to be. A source of insight for the business is also the observation of how data changes over time.

Storing data at the grain of change, as discrete events, allows the system to never forget. The decision of what to expose in the GraphQL API can be made at a later point in time. The event materializer can rematerialize events as requirements change for what is exposed in the GraphQL schema. Data is never discarded by default, even though it may not initially be visible.

Message Driven

In being message driven, the system is aligned with the fundamental principles of the Reactive Manifesto that I discussed in the third chapter. Exchanging messages is also a sometimes-overlooked core concept of object-oriented programming. Some interactions with the GraphQL API will be synchronous, such as execution queries and mutations. GraphQL subscriptions tap directly into the underlying message-driven nature of the system. A mutation will generate a command, and the processing of the command is a message-driven flow. If the command is successfully processed it will generate events, more messages, describing what has changed. Those events will be used by the event materializer to update the view model that is used for queries and subscriptions. Interaction with collaborating systems is accomplished by mapping the events into messages to exchange with them.

Read/Write Separation

GraphQL's separation of queries, subscriptions, and mutations provides the basis for separating reads and writes. Writes are accomplished with mutations, which generate commands and feed the command processor. These components are not used in the system's read path, which only needs to interrogate the output of the event materializer. While reads and writes may both be exposed via the same GraphQL schema, the internal implementation paths are discrete, following the ideas of CQRS. The degree to which the underlying infrastructure is separate then becomes a deferrable implementation decision. The system's architecture is already amenable to this separation.

Partial Availability

At a high level, partial availability is closely related to the separation of reads and writes. With reads and writes taking discrete paths within the systems, they may fail independently without compromising the system (although the value of a system that is available for writes only may be dubious in some situations). The use of message passing via the command and event logs allows either the producers or consumers to fail independently. The logs will buffer messages allowing affected portions of the system to resume their activities after failure. The system is set up to be partially available.

Design Flexibility

As I mentioned when initially discussing design flexibility, it is a squishy topic. There's no specific measure of exactly how flexible a design is. It is something that will be seen over time as the system is able to incrementally evolve rather than requiring wholesale replacement. Business applications can become critical pieces in larger business processes and thus become very entrenched. If business requirements shift in a way that a system's architecture cannot accommodate, the business is then placed in a bind; should it work around the software, or should the more difficult work to either force the change into the system or replace the system entirely be taken?

I believe the proposed design is flexible. The components of the system are loosely coupled, exchanging messages. With the fundamental data storage at the grain of change via events, new events can be introduced as needed. The materialized view of the events isn't a permanent decision and can be adjusted as needed. Even the choice of GraphQL provides flexibility; the schema can be adjusted, or the usage of GraphQL could be removed entirely.

Modularity

Modularity is directly related to design flexibility; it is one of the means of creating a flexible design. The chapters in this section explained the core modules of the system, the command processor, command generator, and the event materializer. Your implementation may require additional modules which will be straightforward to integrate by tapping into the command and event logs. By using message passing as the primary interaction pattern, modules are loosely coupled allowing the design to be flexible.

Testability

As a part of introducing each module that comprises the high-level data flow, I discussed how the module may be tested. I believe this is evidence toward the testability of the system. Chapter 12 discussed testing the composed system using property-based testing. The serialization of concurrent mutations into the command log allows the command processor to be sequential and thus deterministic. The system's design removes the need to test mutation race conditions as they are resolved early when appending to the command log. How to test the system's modules and the entire system itself has been a consideration from the start.

Amenability to Change

This remains my favorite principle, and a phrase that I will often repeat. Systems that are amenable to change survive and thrive for years or even decades. Ones that aren't are discarded and hopefully replaced with ones that are. That depends, of course, that the developers doing the replacement worked on the original implementation and can understand why there was a need to rewrite the system. If a new team of developers is taking over responsibility for an existing system, a common pattern I've seen is for them to embark upon a rewrite without reflecting upon *why* a rewrite is necessary. By skipping that reflection, they may fall into the same trap as the system they are replacing.

Being amenable to change is a culmination of the prior principles. It isn't sufficient to state this alone, the reasons why must be enumerated. A well-tested system can be changed without fear of introducing unintended behavior changes. A modular system allows for incremental extension and replacement, constraining the blast radius of changes. Partial availability provides bulkheads when something inevitably goes wrong. The principles here support and buttress each other to create a resilient system that I believe is amenable to change.

You now understand how the system's design supports the constraints and principles that we wish the system to have. The next section explores the technologies that will be depended upon to craft an implementation.

Required Technologies

There are a handful of technologies that will be required to implement the described system. As I have described each module of the system, your mind may have already started thinking about how the module may be implemented. This part of the book has focused on the design, and the following discussion of the technologies remains at that higher level. The broad characteristics of the technology are described without yet matching them with an implementation, the subject of the final part of this book.

Append-Only Log

An append-only log is a data structure that represents a sequence of entries with the sole write operation being appending new entries at the end of the log. More succinctly this is a log, but I find adding the *append-only* qualifier helpful when discussing with others.

The command, event, and processed command logs instances of this type of log within the system. While each of these logs stores a different type of message, the fundamental behaviors are the same.

As messages are appended to a log they are assigned a strictly increasing sequence number; these do not need to be contiguous integers. The log must support appending multiple messages as a part of a transaction.

Transactions must have the standard ACID properties, atomicity, consistency, isolation, and durability. In the context of our system, writing multiple messages should be atomic. The only required invariant for consistency is the assignment of strictly increasing sequence numbers to each message. Only the command log will receive concurrent writes, so there will be concurrent transactions that must be isolated from each other. The order in which commands are appended to the log defines the order that they will be processed in. When a batch of events is committed to the log, successful completion of the transaction indicates that they are durably stored.

For reads, there are two cases to support. The first is a read over the entire log and the second is seeking a specific sequence number and reading from that position onward. While the second may be emulated using a read over the entire log, filtering out messages less than the specified sequence number, native support for seeking is desirable as it aligns with how the materialization engine interacts with the log when the system starts.

Pub/Sub Messaging

Pub/Sub is shorthand for publish/subscribe. A pub/sub messaging system is one where there may be multiple publishers and multiple subscribers. When a message is published, it is delivered to all subscribers. There is no defined order for messages and each subscriber *may* see discrete orderings. Messages are ephemeral. If a subscriber leaves then any undelivered messages are lost. A subscriber will not receive messages that were published prior to their arrival. All subscribers must receive messages that are published while they are present.

The append-only message logs manifest within the system as infinite logs. Read operations never end, instead waiting for new messages and emitting them upon arrival. As this may not be a native feature for an append-only log, it is called out as a discrete technology requirement as it may be constructed by combining the append-only log with pub/sub messaging. After the commit of an append operation to the message log, the writer publishes a message indicating that the log has new messages. This allows the application-level manifestation of the message log to subscribe to the pub/sub messages and use those messages as triggers to re-query starting from the last-observed sequence number.

The materialization engine also makes use of pub/sub messaging. When the materialization engine updates the view for a given domain identifier, it can publish a message indicating that the update has occurred. GraphQL subscriptions are backed by these updates; each GraphQL subscription is a transient subscription to the updates. When an update occurs, it may result in a new message being sent on the subscription. A message on a GraphQL subscription is not guaranteed because there is a disconnect between exactly what data was updated in the view and exactly what the GraphQL field selection set contains. While the view updates may be made more granular, I find that this is generally diminishing returns in system complexity. There must be enough updates that would result in a material amount of work to determine if there is an update to send. It is good to be cognizant of this decision, and I prefer to monitor and address as necessary, rather than undertaking more work from the start.

Distributed Locking

The system's design isn't restricted to a single application instance. When deployed to a cloud environment, it *should* be run as multiple instances for resiliency. Deployments will also have multiple versions of the application running as new instances come into service prior to destroying old ones. While any instance will be able to serve read traffic, the system's design assumes that the command processor and materialization engine are singletons, running on a single instance.

In order to prevent multiple instances from running these modules, we require a mechanism for distributed locks. The command processor and materialization engine will be guarded by their own locks, allowing them to each to run on different instances, while only allowing at most one instance to run each. Each instance will have a background process that is continually trying to acquire the lock, and if successful, will start the guarded module. When an instance terminates, the lock will be released allowing another instance to take over that responsibility.

Your implementation may have additional modules for your domain that also need to act as singleton processes, and the same distributed locking implementation should be reusable for those purposes as well.

Database

The materialization engine needs to materialize the view into a database. The specific type of database that you decide to use will depend upon your domain data and what you are comfortable operating. Some domains may be amenable to document databases, where entities are coarse and maintaining a single document per entity matches the read characteristics. Other domains may want to use a relational database as their ubiquity has led to many developers being familiar with them. Your domain and business rules may require the materialization engine to perform aggregations that are well-suited to the relational model.

There is no one-size-fits-all, and the technology you choose here will depend upon your situation. A benefit of this system's design is that the decision of which database to use is not a permanent one; this is our amenability to change principle. The authoritative store for your data is in the append-only event log. Multiple materialization engines can maintain multiple views if you choose to transition to a new store.

Summary

You now understand how the proposed design is aligned with and supported by the system constraints and operating principles. There's a small number of technologies required for implementation, pub/sub messaging, distributed locking, an append-only log, and a database for the materialized view. I hope that the gears in your head are turning, thinking about implementations of these that you are comfortable working with. This concludes the section of this book on the system's design. The next section and chapter dive explore an implementation.

PART IV

Implementation

CHAPTER 14

Building with Modern Spring, Java, and PostgreSQL

In our journey so far, I've explained this book's definition of business applications, the properties and features that are desirable in business applications, and introduced a design that satisfies those properties and features. While the prior parts of this book have been implementation agnostic, this final part is focused on implementing the design with specific technologies.

In this chapter, I introduce the set of tools that I have used to implement the design. I hope that you will appreciate my choices.

Required Technologies via PostgreSQL

The prior chapter mentioned four key technologies needed to implement the design:

- Append-Only Log
- Pub/Sub Messaging
- Distributed Locking
- Database

All these technologies may be fulfilled with a single solution, PostgreSQL. It is a robust database system that has been under active development for more than 30 years, available as open source under its own liberal license that is similar to the BSD or MIT licenses. I first started using it in the year 2000 when it was the only open source

P. Royal, *Building Modern Business Applications*, https://doi.org/10.1007/978-1-4842-8992-1_14

relational database system that supported ACID transactions and foreign keys. Its strong focus on reliability and data integrity drew me to the project and it has become my database system of choice for projects that require one.

When designing systems, I like to minimize the operational overhead. If each of the technologies were solved by a separate implementation, that would be five stacks to wrangle (the four technologies plus the application itself). With the current trends where teams practice DevOps and are responsible for both development and operations, this minimization of operations responsibilities allows teams to ultimately be more agile.

If PostgreSQL becomes a limiting factor for one of these technologies, the option of swapping the implementation is always available. This harkens back to two of our principles: design flexibility and modularity.

From another perspective, one of the technologies *is* a database. If the database also has other capabilities available out-of-the-box, why not also use those? I once had teammates that advocated for using discrete tools, arguing that a tool that has multiple functions is akin to a "spork," a type of hybrid cutlery that functions as a spoon and a fork. Sporks are often looked down upon, as most encounters are with single-use sporks as a part of fast-food or prepackaged meals. In those situations, the usage of a spork is often a cost-cutting and waste-reduction measure to provide a single utensil rather than two. The choice of a spork was imposed. My counterargument is that sometimes one may choose to use a spork. If you are going camping and want to minimize the number of utensils that you are carrying, the consolidation of functions into a single utensil is now a desirable feature, and it is a decision that you made for yourself.

In the following sections, I will elaborate upon how PostgreSQL is able to satisfy all the requirements.

Advisory Locks

Like many databases, PostgreSQL internally uses locks in order to provide its consistency guarantees. Under normal circumstances, this is generally transparent to users. You'll be aware of them when debugging problems, such as statements that aren't completing as expected due to them waiting on locks.

PostgreSQL exposes the ability to create locks that have application-defined meaning. These locks are called *advisory locks* because from the database server's perspective they have no semantic meaning, and the server doesn't enforce their usage.

There are two varieties of advisory locks, locks that are bound to a transaction and locks that are bound to a connection (the PostgreSQL documentation refers to this as a *session*). Locks can also be shared or exclusive; we want to use exclusive locks as the goal is to obtain an exclusive right to run a process in the application cluster.

If you are thinking that locks may be emulated with a flag in a table, you are correct. There are two advantages to using advisory locks. The first advantage is that lock activity is kept outside of the structures that PostgreSQL uses to store table data. PostgreSQL uses a multi-version concurrency control (MVCC) model where updates to rows don't modify data in place. Instead, they create a new version of the row that is only visible to newer transactions. As older transactions are complete, there will be rows that are no longer visible by any transaction and can be cleaned up. This is the essence of vacuuming, a critical background maintenance process that is often transparent but important to be aware of. The second advantage is a critical one that I believe tilts the table in favor of using advisory locks; they are automatically released when the obtaining transaction or connection completes (depending on the type that was acquired).

For our system, we will use advisory locks that are bound to a connection. When the connection terminates (whether intentionally or not), we have a server-provided guarantee that an acquired lock will be released.

When attempting to acquire a lock there are two basic patterns that may be used. The first is to use a blocking call where the lock acquisition blocks until it can be obtained. I'm not a fan of this method because the blocking statement manifests as a long-running SELECT statement; lock manipulation is done via function calls that are invoked with SELECT's. I find that the long-running statements distort monitoring of the system as they need to be filtered out given that they are expected behavior. Long-running statements may also not generate any network activity from the caller which can also cause the underlying TCP connection to be timed out in some environments. This can be especially pernicious to debug!

My preferred pattern is to use the lock acquisition function that tries to acquire and immediately returns a boolean result that indicates if acquisition was successful. This allows my code to control how often lock acquisition is attempted, usually every 5 to 10 seconds. I prefer this because it avoids both problems from the prior paragraph; the acquisition attempts run deterministically, and the connection is exercised on each attempt preventing it from appearing unnaturally idle.

Once a lock has been acquired the connection does need to be exercised to ensure that is healthy. To achieve this, I execute a SELECT 1 call every few seconds in a loop. If you aren't familiar with this idiom, it is the same statement that connection pools use to validate the health of a PostgreSQL connection; it returns the literal value 1. If the connection has been unexpectedly terminated, the statement will fail allowing our code to react to the termination.

LISTEN and NOTIFY

PostgreSQL contains a publish/subscribe (pub/sub) messaging system in the form of the LISTEN and NOTIFY commands. Messages are organized into channels and can contain an optional payload. The NOTIFY command is used to send a message, and LISTEN is used to listen for messages.

NOTIFY

For publishing, a pattern suggested by the PostgreSQL documentation, and the one that I also use, is a trigger attached to a table to generate messages. This can be combined with PostgreSQL's JSON functions to pass the updated row as JSON back to the application. Here's an example snippet that I'll use to explain further:

```
CREATE FUNCTION send_notification()
    RETURNS TRIGGER AS
$$
BEGIN
    PERFORM pg_notify('my_channel_name', row_to_json(new)::TEXT);
    RETURN NULL;
END;
$$ LANGUAGE plpgsql;

CREATE TRIGGER notify_table_updated
    AFTER INSERT OR UPDATE
    ON your_table
    FOR EACH ROW
EXECUTE FUNCTION send_notification();
```

Starting from the bottom, a trigger is attached to a table, in the example it's your_ table. You'll also name the trigger, rather than my placeholder's name of notify_table_ updated. For each row that is inserted or updated, the send_notification function will be invoked. This is boilerplate for creating a trigger on a table; the action to perform is separate from creating the trigger on a table as this allows the function to be reused across multiple tables.

The send_notification function is the action. It is a function defined as a trigger. It performs a single task, invoking the pg_notify function. This function is equivalent to the NOTIFY command; it is used instead of NOTIFY as is easier to use with nonconstant channel names or payloads, which the example is doing. The channel name is my_channel_name with a payload being a JSON representation of the modified row. In triggers, new refers to the new state of the data and we pass that to row_to_json to convert it to JSON, followed by a cast back to TEXT as that's the datatype required by pg_notify.

Another benefit of using NOTIFY is that it is transactional. Messages sent within a transaction are not delivered until the transaction has committed. If the transaction is rolled back, nothing ever delivered.

There is also nothing wrong with explicitly calling NOTIFY from application code. I prefer the trigger approach for most usages as the event is often related to data changes in a table and coupling it to the table within the database ensures that they are always generated. There are situations where I want to send messages that are unrelated to table changes, such as passing heartbeat messages across the cluster.

LISTEN

For subscribing, the LISTEN command is used. It takes a single parameter, the name of the channel to listen on. A connection may listen to multiple channels at once.

As this functionality is outside of the SQL standard, access to events is a proprietary feature in PostgreSQL drivers. It isn't exposed in the database agnostic APIs that many platforms offer.

A connection that is LISTEN-ing should be dedicated for this purpose. The returned data structure will vary slightly according to the client API in use, but a commonality with all of them will be access to the channel name and payload.

I'll discuss LISTEN in more depth later in this chapter as a part of introducing the R2DBC API.

Schemas

PostgreSQL provides a layer of organization within a database in the form of schemas. Database objects such as tables, types, and functions always exist in a schema. If you've used PostgreSQL before, you may have seen references to `public`, the default schema that all databases have, and the one that tables as other objects will be created in by default. There's a runtime parameter named `search_path` that controls which schemas to search for objects in. By default, it includes `public` which is why you can write `SELECT * FROM my_table` rather than `SELECT * FROM public.my_table`.

The first benefit from schemas is for authorization. Since we will be using PostgreSQL for multiple functions, we can use schemas to organize objects and grant access. Our system will be using PostgreSQL to store the command log, event log, and our materialized view for queries. Each of these will be a separate schema, and then we can create read-and-write roles for that schema that different aspects of our code can use when accessing the database. Schemas aren't strictly required to do this, but they assist with maintenance as privileges can be granted at the schema level, alleviating the need to explicitly enumerate each object within the schema.

The second benefit is allowing the reuse of table names. Database object names only need to be unique *within a schema*. Think of the contents of a schema as an interface. A schema that's acting as an event log will have certain objects inside of it. If another event log is desired, a new schema can be created with the same contents. The application code can be entirely reused, the only change needed would be to change the `search_path` runtime parameter of the connection to include the desired schema name.

I find this to be even *more* powerful when combined with the materialization engine. Imagine a scenario where a new version of the application needs to make a backward-incompatible change to the tables used to satisfy reads from the system (if it's possible to be backward compatible, always prefer that). The read model can be rebuilt into a new schema with new application code using a new schema inside of the database. If the application code needs to be rolled back, it is straightforward as the model used by the prior version still exists in the prior schema. The new model can be materialized in the background, with the older code serving reads from the older model until the new code has materialized the new schema. At that point, the old code is taken out of service and the new code serves read requests.

Append-Only Log

Using PostgreSQL for an append-only log is straightforward; it's a table! The append-only feature can be achieved by using PostgreSQL's authorization system and denying the ability to update or remove rows. The other features we want from an append-only log, ACID transactions and the ability to query some or all the rows are already features of PostgreSQL.

PostgreSQL is a feature-rich database system. I believe it is an excellent starting point for most projects and will be sufficient for the lifetime of many more. In this section, I've explained my reasoning for using it to satisfy all four of the required technologies for our system. In the next section, I'll move "up to the stack" so-to-speak and discuss my choice for the application layer where our business logic will live.

Java and the JVM

The Java Virtual Machine (JVM) has proven to be an extremely capable runtime platform for business applications. It has a mature ecosystem of tools for packaging software, debugging, and performance monitoring. There is also a vibrant community of open source development with libraries and frameworks available to assist with many of the tasks you may encounter.

While other languages are available for the JVM, I've found the Java language to be my preferred choice. The language designers take a pragmatic approach to adding new features, preferring to think deeply around how they interact with an understanding that code written against them will be in service for many years. I believe this deliberate pace to changes is one reason why alternate languages have sprouted up, such as Groovy, Scala, and Kotlin. While each of these may offer a short- or medium-term productivity boost, I do not think they are the best choices for software systems that may have a lifetime of a decade or more.

Comparisons between Java and COBOL have been made, with a meme of *Java is the new COBOL*. While the two languages are very different, the role of the *de-facto enterprise language* has shifted from COBOL to Java.

Java also has a strong commitment to backward compatibility. Code compiled and written for earlier versions of the language continues to compile and execute on newer versions of the JVM (modulo the code's authors using public APIs). I believe this is very important for business applications as this helps minimize the required maintenance for systems.

153

No programming language is perfect (although I suspect some proponents of LISP would argue that it is). Java is a pragmatic choice. If you are more comfortable with another language or runtime, implement this system using that. I do implore you to consider the expected lifetime of your work, realizing that it will likely be longer than you think if it ends up being successful. Are you setting at best, your future self, or at worst, someone new entirely, up for a migration off an abandoned language or runtime? It is this line of thinking that keeps me on Java and the JVM. It has a proven track record of being used for over two decades.

GraphQL-Java

GraphQL has a robust specification. It defines the language, type system, how validation is performed, and the execution model to use. The level of detail that it contains is beneficial for users of the technology as it allows producers and consumers to understand expected behavior.

The flip side of having this level of detail in the specification is that it is not amenable to one-off implementations. Thankfully, there are open source implementations of the specifications in many languages. In 2015 Andreas Marek started the GraphQL-Java project and it has become the leading implementation for Java. It is a focused library that mirrors the focus of the GraphQL specification. The library manages *only* execution of GraphQL documents, leaving the concern of how the code communicates with other systems up to users. This combined with the codebase's focus on minimizing additional third-party dependencies make it a sound choice to build upon.

There is also a synergistic implementation decision within the library. Recall our self-imposed constraint of wanting to be real time and achieving that using GraphQL's subscriptions. GraphQL-Java's implementation of subscriptions uses the Reactive Streams, `www.reactive-streams.org`, specification. Reactive Streams is an effort to provide a standard for asynchronous stream processing in the vein of the Reactive Manifesto and the type of reactive systems that we are constructing. GraphQL-Java has a dependency on an API, not an implementation. In the next section, I will be explaining Reactive Streams in more depth.

Spring Boot

The Spring Framework has been a part of the Java ecosystem since 2002. At the time, it was a simpler alternative to the Enterprise JavaBean programming model that was promoted by Sun Microsystems, the creator and steward of Java at the time. Spring has adapted to changes in how Java applications have been architected and packaged. Prior to the rise of microservice architectures in the end of the 2000s, developers packaged their code and deployed it into running application servers such as Apache Tomcat, JBoss, or IBM's WebSphere (to name a few). These were multi-tenant systems often managed by central teams. Contemporaneous with the rise of microservices was the advent of DevOps, a practice where developers were responsible for the full lifecycle of their systems, including operations. DevOps is very related to the Agile and CI/CD practices mentioned in the second chapter of this book.

In the early 2010s, Spring Boot was created. It inverted the relationship that the Spring Framework had with application servers. Instead of deploying code into an application server, the necessary portions of an application server (often only the HTTP server) were embedded inside of a Spring Boot application, putting control of the process lifecycle into the hands of developers. Over the past decade, Spring Boot has become the primary way that the Spring Framework is consumed. It has easy-to-use patterns to enable developers to rapidly assemble and maintain applications.

Like Java and the JVM, the Spring maintainers value backward compatibility and strive to maintain this within major releases. My perspective is that Spring is curating a set of well-thought-out abstractions. By building against these abstractions, our code is shielded from changes in implementation details. I value this as a practice in my own work, as I believe it is an important part of building systems that are amenable to change which is one of the guiding principles of the system that this book describes. Spring does evolve faster than Java, and there is a corresponding faster pace of deprecations in some areas as abstractions are refined. The guiding principles in this book again help here. By ensuring that our system is modular, testable, and amenable to change, the process of adapting to changes in the framework that the system is built upon has parallels to the process of adapting to changes from the business. The principles behind Spring Boot are aligned with ours, and I have found it to be an excellent starting point for my work.

Project Reactor

I discussed the four properties from the Reactive Manifesto and how they can be composed to create reactive systems in Chapters 3 and 4. These ideas begat a set of abstractions for use by implementors in the form of Reactive Streams. Recall from Chapter 3 that I said that being message driven is the most important property from the manifest. It is this property that the specification enables. Streams are composed of discrete messages, and the specification formalizes low-level interaction patterns by introducing the concepts of a `Publisher` and a `Subscriber`. In Chapter 3, I also discussed how the manifesto's properties are composable. I view the Reactive Streams specification as the smallest unit in a composition hierarchy, allowing systems that are built around this specification to exhibit these properties through-and-through.

Reactive Streams are sometimes misconstrued. The usage of the reactive programming model is sometimes believed to be only for the benefit of systems that operate under high load and want to use asynchronous message passing to reduce the total number of threads with the goal of optimizing utilization of the available hardware. While this is certainly a reason to use Reactive Streams, this is not the rationale for our business applications. We are valuing the composition of the message passing paradigm across all layers of the system. Effective usage of compute resources is a beneficial side effect and not the primary goal. I am valuing building a fully reactive system and minimizing impedance mismatches that can arise from mismatched paradigms.

The Reactive Streams specification is at a lower level than we will want for usage with our application's design. Thankfully, we do not need to implement the specification ourselves. Project Reactor is an implementation of the specification in Java and is also the implementation used by the Spring Framework and integrated into Spring Boot. Reactor provides many stream operations such as `map` and `filter`, allowing us to focus on writing code that uses Reactive Streams without needing to implement stream processing primitives.

Project Reactor provides implementations of a Reactive Streams `Publisher` that is enhanced with static methods to initiate streams and instance methods to apply stream operations. Because the `Publisher` specification defines it as a stream of unspecified length, Reactor splits its API surface into two categories. Streams that are known to be at most a single element are represented as a `Mono` with all others being represented as a `Flux`. This is beneficial because the `Mono` type is analogous to the `CompletableFuture` API that is part of the Java standard library and Reactor provides methods to interoperate between the two.

In Chapter 3, I introduced a pipe metaphor for data flows. Project Reactor is the implementation of those pipes. Reactive Streams defines how segments of the pipes interact. It formalizes the semantics for publishing and subscribing, cancellation, and flow control.

The ability to think in data flows is what drew me to Reactive Streams and Project Reactor. It is very important to note that the abstraction has a leak around the threading model. As of the writing of this book, the JVM maps threads directly onto operating system threads. Care should be taken to limit the number of JVM threads that are executing in parallel, as having this number exceed the underlying hardware's capabilities will result in a degraded experience. Thinking in data flows *should* allow developers to not worry about these implementation details, and in the general case that is true. You need to be aware of code that may be executing blocking operations, such as performing I/O, as that can cause stalls. There is active work to add virtual threads to the JVM as a part of Project Loom. When completed, virtual threads will allow the JVM to efficiently manage very large numbers of threads and fix this leaky abstraction. Some feel that this will negate the need for libraries such as Project Reactor, but I disagree. Data flow programming via Reactive Streams and Project Reactor, as I am describing here, will continue to be valuable irrespective of the underlying implementation. This work in the JVM should *increase* adoption, as many of the complaints leveled against the current implementations will be solvable.

I am mentioning this important detail as there is a very popular blocking API that is widely used with business applications, the Java Database Connectivity API (JDBC). In realizing the value of extending the Reactive Streams paradigm through to the database, a new API was created, the Reactive Relational Database Connectivity (R2DBC) API.

R2DBC

The R2DBC API was created to extend reactive programming through to interacting with relational databases. JDBC requires a thread per connection, and efficiently managing connections within reactive systems can be tricky. By creating a specialized API, Reactive Streams' flow control can be propagated through to database servers.

I find a key value proposition of using R2DBC to be its reactive API. This removes the need to wrap JDBC and the associated care that must be taken to ensure the safe usage of its blocking API. I have done that in the past with success but am happy to no longer need to do so with R2DBC.

The PostgreSQL driver for R2DBC has one feature that makes me very happy – the ability to get the results of a LISTEN command as a Project Reactor Flux. This allows PostgreSQL's pub/sub messages to be consumed as messages within a Reactive Stream within our application.

jqwik

There is an excellent library for property-based testing in Java, jqwik.[1] It is another engine for the widely used JUnit 5 platform, allowing you to incorporate its use alongside other example-based tests that also use the platform. jqwik has first-class support for generating a series of actions to perform which make it an ideal candidate to drive the type of tests I described in Chapter 12. Each mutation will have an associated action. When invoked, an action is provided with a state object that you define. This state object acts as the oracle. An action will invoke its mutation, and upon success also update the oracle. The action can then can a GraphQL query to interrogate the current state of the system using the information in the oracle to understand what it should be. To control the order in which actions are called, they can optionally have preconditions. Using the example from Chapter 12, an invoice must exist before being submitted for approval. The action that invokes the mutation to submit for approval will have a precondition that there is at least one invoice that can be submitted. This will prevent jqwik from creating a sequence of actions that is invalid for your domain.

There are two parameters you can control for the exhaustiveness of the tests, the number of actions to perform and the number of times to perform the actions. If you wanted to run 100 actions, you could have one attempt with 100 actions, or 4 attempts of 25 actions. The proper balance will depend upon the nature of your domain, but I tend to have under 10 attempts with 10's of actions. I balance the number of attempts and actions in each test run against the time it takes in my build system. If you are practicing continuous delivery and building multiple times a day, shorter build times may be of value to you.

Another reason to prefer small numbers of actions is when you inevitably reproduce a failure. When a jqwik test fails, the output includes a seed value that can be used to reproduce the same random values. This is why determinism is critical. All randomness in a test run *must* tie back to the seed value for the seed to be useful in reproducing failures.

---

[1] https://jqwik.net

A randomly generated series of actions won't necessarily call all the actions you have defined. In order to ensure that the test exercises what you want it to, jqwik allows you to collect statistics around the actions in each attempt. You can then define success criteria for these statistics that will fail the test if not met. I use this functionality to ensure that each action is invoked at least once in each attempt.

Putting It All Together

The tools I have described in this chapter can be assembled to form a reactive system, as I described in Chapter 3. Additionally, the implementation that is behind the GraphQL façade will also follow the Reactive Streams specification, allowing for a cohesive internal programming paradigm.

The system will utilize three schemas within a PostgreSQL database: one to store commands, another to store events, and the third for a materialized view to handle GraphQL read requests. Just as code is organized into packages to group and isolate concerns, the same approach is taken for objects within the database.

The Spring Framework contains a library that integrates GraphQL-Java with Spring, Spring for GraphQL, that can be used within Spring Boot. Every field defined in a system's GraphQL schema is backed by code that provides the field's data. Most fields will use the default implementation that is able to look up a field's value in common associative structures such as a Map, fields of a class, or methods that follow the JavaBean conventions. These pieces of code are known as a DataFetcher, the name of the functional interface that they must implement. A feature of Spring for GraphQL is that a DataFetcher can return a Project Reactor type such as a Mono or Flux, allowing direct integration of Reactive Streams code with the GraphQL runtime. This allows for straightforward implementations of features such as request deadlines, as well as direct wiring of our metaphorical pipes between internal components.

Our system can be viewed as a loop, an idea I introduced in Chapter 8. The current state of the system is visible by using the read capabilities of the GraphQL schema. A point-in-time snapshot may be obtained by using a query. A subscription can be used to get a point-in-time snapshot followed by additional snapshots as the data changes. To change the state of the system, a mutation can be issued. This mutation is received by the system, and the command generator transforms the mutation's payload into a command. This command is then appended to the command log. The command processor consumes from the command log and processes the command using the mutator and applicator functions in concert with the necessary state to enforce business rules. An output of this process is a processed command which is used to record the command's disposition. This disposition is reflected to the initiator of the mutation. Successful commands also result in a set of events that are appended to the event log. The materialization engine is consuming the event log and incrementally updating a schema within our database that backs the GraphQL read APIs. Each of these steps was described in detail in Part 3 of this book.

Starting with the message logs, reads for each of them can be represented as an infinite Flux containing all current and future messages. There is a straightforward optimization that may be applied to this approach. Most message log consumers will not be consuming the entire log; they will want to start with messages that are after the last message they consumed. This leads to a straightforward API contract for consumers:

```
interface MessageLog<T> {
    Flux<T> messages();

    Flux<T> messagesSinceSequence(long seq);
}
```

Due to the usage of a Flux, this interface can satisfy consumers that want to access a subset of the messages, as well as those that want to subscribe to new messages as they are made available.

The implementation of this interface combines past and future messages from their storage tables. Past data is straightforward; it is a SELECT statement with a WHERE clause that only selects messages greater than a given sequence number. Future messages reuse that same code path by using a call to LISTEN that receives notifications containing new sequence numbers. When a new sequence number is available, if it is greater than the last known value, the SELECT is re-executed returning new messages. Since the call to LISTEN is returning a single value, if values are being generated faster than consumers can process them, applying backpressure is straightforward because only the most recent message needs to be retained, the one containing the new maximum sequence number.

The materialization engine uses the message log containing events, the event log, to maintain the schema within the database that is used to satisfy GraphQL queries. As the materialization engine updates tables, the updates can issue a NOTIFY where appropriate for your domain. These notifications will be listened to by the code that powers GraphQL subscriptions to know when to generate new ticks on the subscription stream. This is the same pattern used by the message logs; LISTEN/NOTIFY is used to notify portions of the system when new data is available.

There will be several DataFetcher implementations for our system. At a minimum, they will exist for each of the fields on the Query and Subscription types as fields there represent entry points into the schema. These implementations will issue queries against the database schema containing the materialized view that is designed to handle these requests. A benefit of this is that there should be little-to-no impedance mismatch between the two schemas.

When designing schemas, I like to reuse the types returned by fields of the Query and Subscription types:

```
type Invoice {
  id: ID!
  customer: Customer
}

type Customer {
  id: ID!
  name: String
  invoices: [Invoice]
}

type Query {
  customer(id: ID!): Customer
}

type Subscription {
  customer(id: ID!): Customer
}
```

Both Query.customer and Subscription.customer return the same data. The only (and important) difference is that the subscription field will return the current state followed by any updated states. This follows the same pattern I mentioned above for implementing a MessageLog; there is a query that can load the data, and notifications received on a LISTEN to the database signal the application to re-execute the query. By reusing patterns, an understanding of one portion of the system applies to others, as well as opening the possibility for sharing implementation code.

Summary

In this chapter, I have introduced the set of tools that I have used to successfully implement the design introduced in the third part of this book. You have learned how PostgreSQL is an ideal database to use as it is able to satisfy all the required technologies from the prior chapter with a single solution. You have also learned that a fully reactive implementation is achievable with Spring Boot, Project Reactor, GraphQL-Java, and R2DBC. The next chapter is devoted to how the design can be extended with additional features and alternate ideas for implementing it.

CHAPTER 15

Expansion Points and Beyond

I started this book by sharing my perspective on how to define business applications. Extending from that definition I then described how to think about building them in order to satisfy a set of properties and features that I feel are valuable to both the business and you, the developer. The design I've introduced has been explained without prescribing any specific implementation. After fully explaining the design in the third part of this book, the prior chapter was an introduction into the set of tools that I have successfully used for implementing the design. In this final chapter, I share some parting thoughts on the philosophy underpinning the system from this book, ideas for extending the core components, and directions that you can take your own implementations.

Design Flexibility and Amenability to Change

If I were to look back at the various software systems that I have worked on, the facet that partitions them into ones that I dreaded working with, and those that were not, was the ease with which changes can be made to the system. This is irrespective of the scope of the changes that I was asked to do. What may seem like a straightforward modification to business logic can be made far more complicated if the system and its environment aren't amenable to change.

This is a property that runs deep within a system. I believe if it isn't incorporated from the outset, it can be extremely difficult to incorporate afterward. This is the basis for the inclusion of how testing can be approached for each of the key components of this book's system. It is also why immutability is preferred wherever possible. I find that code that prefers immutability is easier to reason about, making modifications more

163

© Peter Royal 2023
P. Royal, *Building Modern Business Applications*, https://doi.org/10.1007/978-1-4842-8992-1_15

straightforward. Immutability is also related to the keystone property of the Reactive Manifesto, being message driven. Messages can't be modified once sent; messages are required in order to describe changes.

Software systems will have some amount of inherent complexity. Business workflows are often messy and full of edge cases. As developers, it is our responsibility to the business to minimize the added complexity of our software systems. They should strive to be as complex as necessary, but no more.

A business's needs from its software systems *will* change over time. The software systems we create should have the flexibility to adapt to those changes, and the process of enacting those changes should be straightforward. This is a continual activity over time, and an activity where balance is required. A system that is **too** flexible, often manifesting via high levels of abstraction, can be difficult to change with confidence.

The system described in this book aims to strike this balance. Through thinking about business rule classifications in Chapter 5, the system has specific places for the incorporation of each. This acts as a map, providing guidance to developers as to where different types of changes should be incorporated. The usage of the CQRS pattern, especially when combined with GraphQL's schema language, allows the views of the system's data to evolve independently of how it is mutated. This may seem like extra complexity, especially when beginning a new project. However, if not incorporated at the start, retrofitting a system to add this extension point can be more difficult.

When I was originally iterating on what eventually became the design described in this book, I wanted to minimize fixed decisions. Ideally, every component within the system is replaceable, and again ideally, with minimal disruption to the components it collaborates with. The balance I kept in mind was to think about how it *could* change, but to go no farther. The goal was to not exclude future possibilities while simultaneously not doing more today than is necessary. I can't predict how the needs of the system will evolve.

There are limitations to the architecture presented. It embodies a set of tradeoffs. The sections of this chapter are exercises in utilizing the design's flexibility. Perhaps some of them are important enough to your work that you will want to incorporate them from the outset. There is no one size that will fit all.

Multiple Command Processors

A key simplification present in this book's system is that there is a single command processor. This should not be construed to mean that there is a single command processor for the entire business. In Chapter 1 when introducing this book's definition of business applications, they are both domain-specific, relative to the domain the business operates in, as well as targeting specific departments within an organization. Departments are also domains, such as accounting, sales, or customer support.

Although the underlying paradigms of event sourcing have been used for millennia, their wider usage within software systems is still nascent. When researching event sourcing, you will likely encounter recommendations to limit the number of events within an event log. While this is a fine recommendation grounded in the experience of others, it also adds complexity. The usage of a single command processor and event log is an intentional simplification of the design. The state the command processor maintains in order to enforce business rules is akin to the state that developers may be familiar with maintaining in a relational database. The code that enforces rule-keeping has full access to all the system's data. This minimizes the conceptual differences in moving from mutating data in place to the command processor approach.

The incorporation of multiple command processors was a future possibility that I kept in mind during initial ideation. I think there are multiple ways to think about this depending upon your goals.

There could be a single command log and a single command processor. Events, however, could be tagged with a value that can be used as a partition key. This would allow the consumers of the event log to limit the events they receive. If your system's bottleneck is related to event consumption, this may be a viable approach.

A single command processor is a bottleneck for the write throughput that the system can support. If mutations arrive in bursts, a single command processor may still be sufficient depending upon how long it takes to process the backlog. If allowing a queue to build would violate your system's responsiveness objective, or if the mutation rate would prevent a single command processor from ever catching up, multiple command processors can be created.

If multiple command processors are used, it is likely that they may be chained together. Consider a system that manages customers. It is possible to add new customers to the system in addition to the maintenance of data for new customers. The business rules of this system have a constraint for customer uniqueness. Each customer has a unique tax ID and adding a customer with a tax ID that is already used by another should fail. All other business rules are scoped to a single customer. To enforce this uniqueness constraint using this book's components, the addition of new customers and the modification of tax IDs need to be maintained by a single command processor, the global rule maintainer. Each customer can then have their own command processor for the maintenance of customer-specific information.

The system will need to use the events from the global rule maintainer's event log to determine the set of known customers and manage the customer-specific command processing engines. Incoming mutations will be dispatched to the appropriate command log. The chaining I mentioned is related to how the creation of a new customer may be implemented. The global rule maintainer is responsible for the known set of customers and their tax IDs. The exposed mutation for creating a customer allows specifying the tax ID in addition to other customer metadata. The event log from the global rule maintainer only contains events relating to the set of customers; all customer details should exist within the per-customer event log. In order to ensure this, the command generator would need to submit a command to the global rule maintainer and await the response, and then submit another command to the customer-specific command log.

This adds complexity to the internals of the system. It is also complexity that can be hidden within the exposed interfaces of the system. This change can be done later in the system's lifespan without requiring changes by the system's callers, as well as without any modifications to the tests of the composed system from Chapter 12.

Another reason to move to multiple command processors may be to address startup speed. A command processor maintains the necessary state for business rule enforcement in memory. This means that all events are replayed from storage whenever the system starts. Multiple command processors allow for the parallelization of that work, but there is another approach: the caching of this state across application starts.

Command Processor State Caching

The command processor maintains the state necessary to enforce business rules, the rules for data at rest. Although this state is a subset of what is contained in the event log, as described in Chapter 9, the command processor reads the entire event log when starting to rebuild this state using your provided applicator function.

This is beneficial because it allows you to change the behavior of the applicator, if, as an example, you need to start tracking additional data from existing events to enforce new business rules.

As your system is in production, and the event log continues to grow, the time required to rebuild this state will increase. Eventually, it may increase to a point where this duration is undesirable for your use-case. This is an excellent metric to track in your implementation, how this duration changes over time. You can use the rate of duration increased combined with a projected rate of growth of the event log to forecast how long this may take into the future. This will allow you time to appropriately prioritize any changes.

The prior section described how multiple command processors may be introduced, which may be a solution for your domain. Not all domains are amenable to partitioning the problem space in a way that would limit the growth of an individual event log over time. In some cases, the pragmatic, or as I like to sometimes say, the least-worst, solution may be to cache the command processor's state.

I am explicitly using the word *cache* rather than *snapshot*. Snapshot can carry the connotation that the information is durably persistent and may be considered an alternate source of truth. That is **not** the case here. Storing the command processor's state across application runs is a performance optimization only. The cached state can be thrown away at any time and the system will continue to perform as expected, only with an increase in the time it takes to restart a command processor.

When caching the command processor's state, it should be done after durably writing events to the event log. If storing the state fails, it should not be fatal to the system. When a command processor starts, rather than starting from the beginning of the event log, using the applicator to reduce each event into a new state instance, it will first load the cached state, and use the last event that it had incorporated to determine where to start consuming from the event log. It would be feasible to only persist the cached state at a time-based interval, as consuming a small number of events at startup should not present a problem.

It is important to have the ability to version the cached state. If the applicator function changes between versions of your code, the existing cached state should not be used so that the state can be rebuilt using the newer applicator implementation. You will need to weigh whether this should be an explicit, developer-driven version, or implicit, using metadata about the code to create stable version numbers.

Caching can also be used in concert with multiple command processors to improve the start time of an individual processor.

A risk to be aware of is the failure mode of being in a position where you have cached state that is unusable, and a command processor that does not start in a sufficient amount of time. A command processor's startup time should be tracked. If it is projected to reach a point where the startup time is untenable, work should be done to improve the system in ways where losing the cached state won't cause problems. In many scenarios, I anticipate that to be the addition of multiple command processors to partition the event log into multiple, smaller, event logs. Using multiple event logs also removes some complexity for materializing events in parallel.

Parallel Event Materialization

The event materializer consumes from the event log in order to maintain a stateful view model that will be used to satisfy GraphQL requests or maintain additional stateful models for other purposes. It can mux multiple message logs together, the event log from a command processing engine being one, materializing the merged set an event at a time.

For callers of the system to observe changes from their mutations, they need to wait for the event materializer to have materialized the events from their command. If this duration is too long, either directly from the amount of work being performed, or indirectly from other callers issuing their own mutations, something will need to be done to reduce this duration.

An approach that may be used is to allow the event materializer to materialize multiple events in parallel. Again, owing to the system's design flexibility, there are multiple paths to achieve this.

If you wish to keep the change wholly located inside of this component, you can use the internal knowledge of the work performed by an event's materialization function to construct ad-hoc partitions. These partitions would be constructed such that the event materializer would first place incoming events into a partition, and then have multiple component-local processes that consume from the partitions in parallel. An advantage to this approach is that the partitions are wholly ephemeral. The partitioning strategy can be changed as needed without any impact to persisted data. A downside to this approach is that checkpointing becomes more complicated. The current position in a message log can no longer be stored as a single value, the last materialized sequence number. Instead, checkpointing will need to maintain the set of materialized sequence numbers. Under ideal circumstances it should converge upon maintaining a single value per message log. An implementation will need to handle tracking the non-linear progress through a message log.

Alternatively, parallelization of the event materializer can leverage multiple command processors. All the approaches described in the earlier section share the same implementation. Multiple command processors are also not strictly required; from the event materializer's perspective, there is no material difference between multiple event logs and representing other sources of data as a message log for materialization. The primary, and perhaps only, difference will be the creation of the event materializer itself. Other sources of data are likely to be known at development time, and an implementation may statically configure the event materializer with the set of message logs to consume from. If multiple command processors are in use, the events from your service will then be spread across multiple event logs. If the number of command processors is dynamic, the event materializer will also need to be able to support dynamically discovering new event logs to materialize at runtime.

Checkpointing itself does not get more complex, as tracking progress across multiple message logs was a feature in the original design. This change may impact callers though. Recall that a successful mutation returns a single value, visibleAsOfRevision, representing the sequence number of the final event when processing the mutation's command.

When using multiple command processors, you will need to decide whether the event sequence number space is shared across all processors, creating a total order across all events, or if sequence numbers are per command processor. Each approach has its merits. If all command processors share the sequence number space, the existence of partitioning in the command processors can be hidden behind the system's external contracts. The semantics of visibleAsOfRevision is unchanged. However, sharing the sequence number space has a coordination cost when generating sequence numbers as well as when waiting for the event materializer. The single scalar value of visibleAsOfRevision does not indicate which event log contained the event. When using checkpoints for read-after-write consistency, it will be necessary to wait for the event materializer to have materialized the revision across *all* the event logs. This is unlikely to be a good long-term solution, but it is a very viable option if multiple command processors and parallel event materialization are added to an existing production system. The existing semantics are preserved, along with the existing performance characteristics. At the cost of changing the mutation response, the single scalar visibleAsOfRevision can be paired with another value that indicates the event log the revision is from. The command generator is reading from the processed command log to determine a mutation's disposition, making this a natural place to store this information. Callers can then provide the pair of values during queries in order to read their writes. If sequence numbers are per command processor, it will be necessary to change the external contract first, requiring callers to provide another value to indicate which event log contains their events.

In any combination of scenarios, there is a migration path toward implementing the parallel materialization of events in an active system.

This and the prior two sections have focused on system changes that can be described as performance improvements. The next three sections describe additional ways of using GraphQL with the system.

Command and Event Logs As GraphQL Subscriptions

The prior chapter introduced a Java interface describing a message log, the generalization of the system's command, and event logs from Chapter 9.

```
interface MessageLog<T> {
    Flux<T> messages();

    Flux<T> messagesSinceSequence(long seq);
}
```

This Java interface can also be expressed in GraphQL.

```
type Message {
    sequence: Int!
}

type Subscription {
    messages(sinceSequence: Int): Message
}
```

GraphQL does not have generics, so I have created a Message type instead of T for the example. GraphQL does not have a Long scalar, owing to its browser-based roots; it is limited to 32-bit numeric values. It is possible to define custom scalar types, which I recommend, to bypass this limitation.

An implementation of the `MessageLog` interface can be backed by code that uses GraphQL subscriptions to consume messages from other hosts. The possibility of doing this without changing the interface speaks to the simplicity and power of both the interface, and the Reactive Streams abstraction that it uses.

All the system's internal message logs can be exposed in this manner. I have found this beneficial in my work for several reasons. The initial impetus to extend the system in this way was to observe the production system. Being able to use standard GraphQL tooling, such as the browser-based GraphiQL IDE, was very valuable. It provides a safe way to observe the incoming commands and generated events. It ensured tight control over the credentials to my production system's database. Developers should not be modifying the datastore of the system directly. The system is making assumptions about the data in the database. For command and event logs, that they are immutable once written. For the stateful view maintained by the event materializer, that it is the only one that is making state changes. Providing access to the message logs as GraphQL subscriptions makes them available for debugging while also ensuring that they are read-only.

These GraphQL subscriptions are also an opportunity for regression testing. Consider the case where extensive changes have been made to the command processor's mutator and applicator functions. While the use of property-based testing introduced in Chapter 12 provides a great deal of confidence, it can sometimes be beneficial to know that what happened in production works as intended.

In a test environment, whether deployed or in a developer's local environment, a command processor can be created that consumes from a command log that is backed by a GraphQL subscription. This is possible because a command contains all the information necessary for the command processor to operate upon it. The test environment's event log can be compared to the production event log to ensure that they are equivalent.

This approach can also be used with the event materializer. While there isn't the same straightforward cross-check on the output, it can be used to ensure that the event materializer is capable of handling all the known events for the system.

As a further extension, a persistent test double of the production system can be created. It would be read-only, not accepting mutations. Instead, it follows the command log from production, processing the same commands and using its own materialization engine. Combined with the two prior techniques, it can be used to provide users with a system that matches production data but exercises newer code.

Exposing the command and event logs for *your* use does not mean they aren't implementation details of the system. They are implementation details and shouldn't be treated as contracts for your collaborators. The next section will discuss how to use these ideas for inter-process communication (IPC) among systems.

Using GraphQL for Inter-Process Communication

Building upon the prior section, we can use the same GraphQL subscription–based approach to explicitly expose data. I touched on this idea in Chapter 11 when introducing the event materializer.

The event materializer can consume from multiple sources. Its implementation contract within your codebase will be to consume from sources that present themselves as a `MessageLog`.

The design in this book is targeted at business applications that manage data for a domain. Often, the lines between domains in a business can be blurry. There may be a system that manages customers, and customers are associated with regions. There may be another system that manages suppliers, and they are also associated with regions. The regions used for customers and suppliers need to be consistent, as the region could be a join key for data analysis. It may make sense to have a third system be responsible for managing regions that is used by both the customer and supplier management systems. If the customer system needs to incorporate region data into the view that the event materializer maintains, it can use a GraphQL subscription to access an event stream from the region management system. For this use-case, the event stream should be a mapped form of the underlying event log. The region management system should use a discrete contract when making itself available to other systems. This reduces coupling among the systems. Changes to the event structure within the region system do not require synchronized changes with users of the GraphQL subscription. They can evolve independently.

In this example, there are relationships between customers, suppliers, and regions. If each system is exposing its own GraphQL endpoint, these relationships aren't directly visible to users of the system. They are spread out across the three schemas. The next section introduces a technique for unification.

Federated GraphQL

Building upon the example from the prior section, imagine that an organization has discrete applications for managing customers, suppliers, and the regions in which they exist. Using the natural boundaries within a larger domain to subdivide it into smaller, often more manageable, units is a central tenet of Domain Driven Design as described in Eric Evan's seminal book, *Domain-Driven Design: Tackling Complexity in the Heart of Software*[1]. Evans describes these units as *bounded contexts*. The departmental view of business applications that this book takes is highly aligned with Evan's definition of a bounded context.

Our example has three systems, which would be three GraphQL schemas that have interrelated concepts. Both customers and suppliers have a relation to the region in which they operate. Imagine a user interface for managing customers that provides the ability to assign customers to regions. This user interface will need region information to display the current state of a customer as well as when allowing users to make changes.

A simple implementation could be to have the UI make calls to each system. While this may seem reasonable in this example of only two systems, think ahead to a more complex domain with a greater number of relationships. The work required in the UI will grow. This has led to the centralization of that work out of the UI code running on user machines into a dedicated backend service for the UI, a pattern known as the *Backend for Frontend* (BFF). A BFF is tailor-made for a single UI. In our example, there may be up to three BFFs, one each for the UI of each domain. The work performed in each will be extremely similar, and again there is an opportunity to remove this duplication.

This duplication was recognized by Apollo,[2] a company providing developer tooling for GraphQL. If each of our domain services, customers, suppliers, and regions, are already exposing a GraphQL endpoint, what if there was a way of describing how the schemas inter-relate and then providing a service that can accept GraphQL requests and appropriately delegate them to other services? This is the essence of Apollo Federation.

Under the Apollo Federation model, each of the three example services would be considered a subgraph. Instead of a BFF, there will be a graph router that combines the subgraphs into a single supergraph. The supergraph service, also known as the router, provides a GraphQL endpoint that exposes the composition of all subgraphs. This service will route incoming requests to the appropriate subgraph service.

---

[1] ISBN 978-0321125217
[2] `www.apollographql.com`

Our example customer system may expose the following in its GraphQL schema:

```
type Customer {
    id: ID
    name: String
    regionId: ID
}
```

It only provides the identifier of the region the customer is in, as that is all the information the service manages. The region system exposes a Region type that contains the name of the region:

```
type Region {
    id: ID
    name: String
}
```

Apollo Federation allows the customer system to expose the following in its schema:

```
type Customer {
    id: ID
    name: String
    region: Region
}
```

Rather than having the customer system expose only the region ID in the schema, it can expose the Region type, even though it is not a part of the customer service. The customer system exposes the following query to access customers:

```
type Query {
    customer(id: ID): Customer
}
```

With Apollo Federation, callers will be able to send queries that cross subgraph boundaries. Here, the name of a region is requested, data that is managed by the region system:

```
query {
    customer(id: "42") {
        id
```

```
    name
    region {
        id
        name
    }
  }
}
```

The router will first route the request to the customer system, loading the customer and the region ID. It will then make another request to the region system to load the ID. The response to the caller obscures the fact that multiple subgraphs were queried, making it appear that the two systems are one. This is akin to the experience that a BFF would provide. However, instead of a UI-specific BFF, the supergraph service is more generalized.

By using GraphQL as the exposed API of your systems, Apollo Federation facilitates the creation of a unified graph acting as a single entry point for all users of all your systems. The act of connecting the schemas of each domain service provides the business with knowledge of how well connected, or not, their schemas are. This knowledge is valuable feedback around data modeling decisions within the organization.

Business applications act as a source of truth for their data and the business itself uses the data to help make decisions. Improving the quality of the data by ensuring it is both modeled and connected appropriately can allow the business to make more informed decisions.

Moving on from leveraging the usage of GraphQL in our system, the next couple of sections explore alternate possibilities for implementing the design.

Outsourcing Distributed System Problems

To implement the architecture described in this book, I enumerated a few required technologies in Chapter 13, append-only logs, distributed locking, a pub/sub system, and a database. Chapter 14 followed with a description of how to use PostgreSQL to meet these needs with a single solution. This is what I have done in my work, and it has proven successful.

This isn't the only path though. There are cross-cutting requirements of distributed systems that can be abstracted out and made reusable. One solution I have prototyped this book's design with is Temporal,[3] an open source platform that allows for the reliable execution of workflows.

In Temporal's model, a workflow is akin to a state machine that is expressed as imperative code. Temporal provides a software development kit (SDK) that helps you ensure that a workflow is written in a deterministic manner. Workflows maintain their own private state. Any actions that interact with state outside of the workflow, such as querying a database or sending an email, are called activities. When a workflow invokes an activity, Temporal manages safe execution of the work by handling timeouts and retries. The workflow can be considered *fault oblivious*, as it is shielded from being concerned with activity failures. This can allow for the succinct expression of a business workflow.

All workflows have a unique identifier, optionally one that you specify. For a given identifier, there can only be one running workflow instance. This behavior makes a Temporal workflow a substitute for how this book's system uses distributed locks.

There are two ways for workflows to communicate. A workflow can send a message to another workflow using a concept Temporal calls signals. When a workflow receives a signal, it can modify its private state in response. The sender of a signal receives no response. If a workflow needs information from another workflow, it can interrogate the other workflow's state using a concept known as queries. Queries are read-only and cannot modify a workflow's state.

The building blocks that Temporal provides, workflows, activities, signals, and queries, are sufficient to implement the three key components of this book's system. The command generator, command processor, and event materializer can all be expressed as Temporal workflows.

Temporal workflows can run forever. This makes them suitable to run both the command processor and the event materializer. Temporal activities can be used to implement reading from message logs, appending to the event log, and updating the stateful view. For the command processor, because the applicator and mutator are pure functions, they are safe to use from within the Temporal workflow. Temporal itself could be used as a means of caching the command processor's state. If the cache needs to be cleared, the workflow can be reset to arbitrary points in time.

---

[3] https://temporal.io/

For the command generator, the handling of each mutation can be a workflow. The client request identifier can be used as a part of the workflow's identifier. The GraphQL layer would initiate a workflow for the mutation passing in the necessary information from the request. It would then await completion of the workflow to return the disposition to the caller. Using Temporal would add additional fault tolerance beyond what I had described in Chapter 10. If the creation of a command requires interaction with other systems, those interactions can be implemented as activities.

Temporal's internal implementation is very similar to the system in this book. The state of a workflow is stored as a sequence of events. If the computer executing a workflow is interrupted, when Temporal restarts a workflow, it reestablishes the workflow's private state by replaying the stored events. Temporal is using event sourcing to manage the state of a workflow. The system I have described in this book uses event sourcing to manage business data.

Temporal is not a database. It would not be appropriate to use it to store the stateful view that is used to satisfy GraphQL queries. The next section introduces a datastore with unique capabilities.

Bitemporal Materialized Views

The system in this book uses the event log as the authoritative source of state for the application. Each event in the event log describes a change. Those changes are used to maintain a stateful view of the system's data using the event materializer. The exact schema of the stateful view will depend upon the data your system is responsible for. Because the events contain all changes over time, it would be useful to query against this dimension.

Think of time in two dimensions. First, there is the time that a change is made to the database. This would be the timestamp of when an event was appended to the event log, or the timestamp of when an event was materialized by the event materializer. This timestamp will be considered *transaction time*, the time when it was processed by the system. The second dimension is *valid time*. This time is a *business domain* concept. The status quo I described in Chapter 2 has many business applications mutating data in place. When mutating data in place, there is no way to retroactively make corrections to data while preserving the fact that a correction was made. Event sourcing and the use of two timestamps, bitemporality, allow for this to be captured. Often, a change's valid time will be equal to the transaction time; information is true when it was recorded.

177

Sometimes, it is useful to record information today that was true as of sometime in the past or will be true at a point in time in the future.

A database that can answer queries as of a valid time, or a database that is able to provide the change history of stored entities would be a powerful addition to the system described in this book. XTDB is one such database. I was drawn to XTDB as their vision[4] is aligned with mine, the use of immutability and persistent storage on disk being cheap.

XTDB is state-centric, whereas this book's system is change-centric. The event materializer is the bridge between those worlds, collapsing the event log's changes into a stateful view. The stateful view it maintains can be stored within XTDB. By using XTDB as the datastore, the GraphQL schema can easily expose the change history of data within the system. It can also allow viewing the state of the datastore at any transaction and valid time combination. If users ever have questions about what the data in the system was at any point in the past, it can be answered. This can be especially powerful if your system powers any review-based workflows where users are primarily concerned with observing changes.

Conclusion

I have enjoyed sharing the design contained within this book with you. I hope that my rationale, principles, and goals resonate with you. Although business applications have been around for decades, the future of software development is still very young. As I explained at the start of this chapter, I believe that durable software systems are designed around an amenability to change. Doing so requires intention, something that may not always be at the forefront of your mind when developing. The importance of solving problems today can obscure the value of being able to solve problems in the future. I believe business systems should take a longer-term view. When a business commissions custom software from developers such as yourself, whether as an employee or contractor, an investment is being made. It is prudent to maximize the return on that investment by building systems in a sustainable way.

I believe the nature of what is sustainable is changing. Persistent storage used to be a scarce and expensive resource. This influenced how applications were built in order to balance the operational costs of a system against the value provided by using more storage. The tradeoffs that a developer would have made decades ago around storage are

---

[4]https://xtdb.com/pdfs/vision-doc.pdf

no longer applicable, but many still write software using those paradigms. Developers are working in new environments and with new capabilities. We need new ideas to go with them.

A goal of mine is for the design described in this book to be durable through the next stage of computing evolution. I realize that I do not know what the future holds. I do know that the work done today needs to be adaptable for what is to come. This is why portions of this book may have felt somewhat abstract; the minimization of implementation details is my attempt at durability. In a way, it is a sort of design flexibility in the book itself. I hope that the intentional abstractness provides you with an opportunity to think about how the ideas will work in your environment. If this book provides you with inspiration to think differently and take your own path, I will see that as a success.

May your work provide value to others and be in service long enough to be considered a legacy.

Index

A

ActiveX, 13
Advisory locks, 148–150
Agile, 16
Apollo Federation model, 173
Append-only log, 140, 153
Append-only message logs, 141
Apple, 14
Apple's WebKit, 14
Application code, 41

B

Backend for Frontend (BFF), 15, 173
Bitemporality, 53, 54
Bitemporal materialized views, 177, 178
Browser-based GraphiQL IDE, 171
Business applications, 175
  agile, 16
  architectures
    consumer applications, 14–16
    green screen, 11
    rich client, 11, 12
    the Status Quo, 9, 10
    web applications, 12, 13
  customer-facing system, 5
  domains, 4
  ERP, 5
  importance, 6
  observability, 18
  TDD, 17

  users, 5
  workflows, 6
  business software, 3, 4
  modern, 7
  CI/CD, 17, 18
Business domain, 177
Business expectations, 31, 32
Business rules, 108
  application developer, 40
  categorizations
    data at rest, 40–42
    derivable data, 44, 45
    side effects, 42–44
  changes
    amenability, 54
    behavior, 54
    data, 54
    event, 55
    time control, 55
  enforcement, 88
  gather requirements, 39
  goals, 39
  human factors and ergonomics, 39
  risk element, 40
Business software, 3, 4

C

Checkpoints, 107
Cloud computing, 7
COBOL, 11

181

Printed in the United States
by Baker & Taylor Publisher Services